INDIAN RIVER JUNI
FORT PIERC

QB
15
R63
1961

9862

A Survey of Astronomy

A SERIES EDITED BY COLIN A. RONAN
ASSOCIATE EDITOR: PATRICK MOORE

There are already many excellent books upon elementary astronomy, and many technical works aimed purely at the expert. Books which form a connecting link between these two standards are rare. In general, the student finds that he has to pass straight from a very elementary volume on to a work which is of a high standard technically, and includes copious mathematical formulæ.

The aim of the present series is to fill this gap in the literature. Some elementary knowledge has been assumed, but the general reader with no specialized knowledge will be able to follow the text, since mathematical formulæ have been used sparingly and, in general, in footnotes or appendices.

Each book has been written by an expert in his specific field, and should be regarded as a 'step' from the elementary to the technical field. Once this series of books has been read and digested, the student should be ready to proceed to more technical volumes. In addition each volume is complete in itself although, of course, the *Survey* will only be complete within the series as a whole.

The series is, then, designed for the benefit of the serious amateur and for the student. It is hoped that University students who are considering taking science degrees will find the books particularly useful.

Throughout the series the design of the volumes has been to give an up-to-date picture, indicating both present advances and also present limitations to our knowledge.

CHANGING VIEWS
OF THE UNIVERSE

by Colin A. Ronan

A SURVEY OF ASTRONOMY edited by Colin A. Ronan

The Macmillan Company · New York · 1961

*First published in the
United States of America, 1961
Copyright © 1961 by Colin A. Ronan
Printed in Great Britain*

To my Father and Mother

CONTENTS

Preface	*page* 9
1 Prehistory	13
2 Early Civilizations	18
3 Greek Ideas – First Phase	37
4 Greek Ideas – Second Phase	56
5 Islam and the Growth of Astronomy in Western Christendom	76
6 The New Approach: I. Dynamics	97
7 The New Approach: II. Observation	124
8 The Twentieth Century	158

APPENDICES

I The Lunar and Solar Calendars	189
II The Epicycle and Deferent and the Movable Eccentric	190
III A Note on the Harmony of the Universe	192
IV Transits of Planets and Determination of the Astronomical Unit	195
V The Celestial Sphere	196
Bibliography	198
Index	201

PREFACE

This book is designed to provide a historical background against which the contemporary picture of astronomical research and endeavour may be drawn. It is not a formal history of astronomy – of which many are already available to the reader – nor is it a formal history of cosmology. Rather it is a sketch of the attitudes with which men have looked at the cosmos. Because these changing views have been conditioned by the varying scientific and religious climate, some assessment has been made of the factors which seem to have lain behind their adoption. G. K. Chesterton once wrote '... A man sees more of things themselves when he sees more of their origin; for their origin is part of them ...', and it is specially important today, when new ideas and concepts of profound importance are being proposed, that the struggles of the past are not forgotten. We must try to see both the achievements and failures, and to appreciate something of the reasons which lay behind them.

In preparing the book the main problem has not been so much what to include but, rather, what to leave out. Other volumes in this series will provide a picture of the astronomical outlook in the mid-twentieth century and, in consequence, only a brief sketch is given of modern times; just enough to provide a back-cloth against which the full picture may be seen in some perspective. On the other hand the astronomy of the Greeks is discussed in some detail in view, not only of the somewhat brief treatment usually provided in most histories, but also because of the singular importance of Greek views on the whole outlook and way of thought which Western civilization has developed. Recent research has made it desirable also to provide a somewhat fuller description than might have been expected of the contributions which came from Babylonia; and some details have also been given of the results of investigations made over the last few years on Aztec astronomy. Finally, it must be remarked that, because of the vital part which photographic methods have played in astronomical observation, a sketch has been provided of the early history of photography.

While writing this book I have been only too well aware of what I owe to those whose writings and lectures have provided me with much food for thought, as well as to those with whom discussions have proved so encouraging. Although it is not possible to thank by name the many persons concerned, I should wish to record here that, without their stimulation, this book would, in all probability, never have been conceived.

London
1960

Changing Views of the Universe

Chapter 1

PREHISTORY

An interest or at least a curiosity in the heavens existed long before Man invented written records. Such evidence as we have is indirect, as indeed it must be. Yet we have only to consider a world before the advent of civilizations, when Man was nomadic, to realize that even the phenomena of night and day must have given cause for wonder. The hot Sun by day and the multitude of stars by night cannot but have intrigued the mind. To these must be added the appearance, disappearance and reappearance of the Moon, which also appeared to change its shape as it travelled on its accustomed journey against the background of the stars. With no artificial lighting, and a life which depended on hunting and fishing to guard against hunger, the heavens were bound to become a subject for study and discussion. The Moon assumed particular importance. The light which it could at times give at night was important to the hunter; its waxing and waning coincided with periodic physiological changes in the adult woman and, in addition, full moon to full moon provided a conveniently short calendar period for Man to use before written records came into use.

Although an entirely nomadic life leaves little time for objective study, early tribes developed quite elaborate taboos and peopled their surroundings with spirits of one kind and another. Magic with its omens and its rites grew increasingly important; sacrifice either for placating powerful spirits or for extracting favours and blessings became widely practised. In due course certain men became set aside as priests and mediators between Man and the spiritual world. Where possible the priest was relieved of the ordinary tribal duties so that he might the better devote himself to carrying out his special activities, and in due course the priesthood came to be the repository of local knowledge. The heavenly bodies continued their cyclic functions, but were ever inaccessible, and it was natural that legends should grow up round them. They appeared to be eternal, whereas Man and his life were but transitory. The Sun, the Moon and the stars then assumed a great significance and were fitted into the scheme of primitive life. The *synodic month*, from new moon to new moon (or full moon to full moon), was brief enough to be conveniently remembered, and for nomadic tribes who had no need to cultivate crops it was a natural calendar. However, when communities settled down, they bred flocks and herds and sowed and reaped. This meant that some seasonal calendar was required which could easily be correlated with annual changes. A calendar based on the apparent passage of the Sun across the sky was needed. Thus the seasonal year came into being. However, there were difficulties. The lunar and solar calendars could not be married together; they are, after all, inherently incompatible. The *tropical* year – the time taken for the Sun to move once through the heavens – is almost eleven days longer than twelve synodic months. True, the two forms of calendar can be correlated over long periods of time, and in due course this was done, necessitated by the fact that in many communities the lunar calendar continued in use for religious festivals. After all, it had 'got in first', and to remove it would appear an act of great impiety. A lunar calendar is even now still used to determine the date of Easter and is a legacy of this idea.[1]

To prepare a solar calendar is not as easy as it seems. It is necessary to follow the Sun's apparent path among the stars, but when the Sun is shining the stars cannot be observed. However, early man no doubt rose with the dawn and prob-

[1] For details see Appendix I.

ably went to bed at sunset, and some genius hit upon the idea of observing the stars just before sunrise and just after sunset, thus finding a means of plotting the Sun's position in the heavens. By this method of heliacal[1] risings and settings the agricultural calendar was computed. Such observations imply a knowledge of the pattern of the stars, and it would seem then that Man early discerned patterns among the 'fixed' stars and so developed constellations, rudimentary though they may have been. Perhaps this is not so surprising as at first sight it may seem. Year after year, from one generation to another, the same patterns of stars presented themselves to man's inquiring gaze, and one might almost expect that some grouping together in patterns would be made. Moreover, legends handed down by word of mouth would be natural pegs on which the patterns could be hung or even formed. Thus from continued observation (or perhaps just 'curious looking') over long periods of time early man built up a simple framework from which he could determine the seasons and regulate life according to his primitive needs. Our earliest definite knowledge of recorded constellation systems are those which were developed separately in Sumeria, Egypt and South America. This does not invalidate the supposition here made; indeed, it shows a widespread need and an equally widespread and similar way of satisfying it.

What were the ideas of primitive man about the cosmos in which he lived? Again there are legends, some fanciful and some fantastic. Something of their ideas can however be reconstructed. What were the stars, and how were they fixed? Obviously they were embedded by some means or other on the inside of a greatdome. One has even now only to get away from city lights and busy roads and stand in the open countryside at night to see the canopy of heaven stretched overhead, and if it were not that we were brought up to know

---

[1] From the Greek '$\eta\lambda\iota\alpha\kappa o\varsigma$ (hēliakos) meaning 'of the Sun'.

otherwise it is likely that we too would have no doubt in our minds that the heavens are a dome. Indeed our superior or, more correctly, our more sophisticated ideas are due to no greater intellect, but to the work of countless individuals who by contributions both great and small have provided a foundation on which others, our immediate predecessors, have built. From these foundations we ourselves can build. We must therefore be cautious before we condemn early man for his naïveté. It is only too easy to be wise after the event. We must take care also that we do not read into the achievements of the past an understanding or, more precisely, an appreciation which they did not possess because of the small store of facts upon which they had to draw. Early man may have thought of the heavens as a dome and no doubt believed the earth to be flat. Yet the question 'what kind of bodies are the stars?' may well never have seriously troubled him. To say they were 'lights' in the sky, or gods, would have sufficed. Nowadays we should turn and ask 'what kind of lights?' and 'how' if lights they are 'do they keep shining for all time?' But we are brought up in an environment which continually questions 'how?' and 'why?' Simpler and far less complete explanations than could satisfy us would in primitive times have sounded entirely satisfactory. An earth which, in spite of local irregularities, could be called flat, together with a dome of heaven, was a noble and notable synthesis, populated though it might be with gods and goddesses.

This then, in outline, appears to be the picture of the universe as early man saw it. His ideas, his traditions, his folklore and legends were handed down by word of mouth, embellishments of one kind or another being added as time went on. Yet whatever may have been the variations from place to place of the general picture of the cosmos, there was excuse for fanciful suggestions. No man could reach up and touch the Sun, the Moon or the stars. No man knew how large or how small they were. Indeed, it is only a hundred years ago that the distances of even the nearest stars were found, and it is not three hundred years since a measure of the Sun's distance was made with any pretensions to accuracy, yet mankind had existed and asked questions about the universe for millennia. However, there is one fact that stands out clearly. Man, in the dim and remote past before the days of written history, recognized the cyclic nature of celestial phenomena. From time immemorial he and his forebears had watched the ceaseless drama of the heavens. The phases of the Moon were regularly repeated. The Sun rose and set, come heat or cold. The stars appeared in their due season with a regularity which was at once both utterly impressive and utterly to be relied upon.

Little wonder, then, that as soon as civilizations began to emerge the philosopher took these regularities for granted and concentrated upon systematizing them, examining the cyclic motions with ever-increasing accuracy. With the advent of definite records in the form of carvings, paintings and hieroglyphs, we can not only be more certain in our knowledge of the past but also can see this development actually taking place. Such information is available for the Egyptians and Sumerians, as well as for other ancient civilizations. Though still incomplete, recent scholarship has broadened our picture of early conceptions of the universe. Early texts still present obscurities and difficulties of interpretation, yet recent research can, nevertheless, lay claim to knowledge of some precision when it comes to the astronomical and cosmological ideas of the great civilizations of millennia ago. It is to these that we must now turn.

Chapter 2

EARLY CIVILIZATIONS

Great civilizations certainly flourished in China, India, South America and the Middle East. All were concerned with the calendar and therefore with astronomical observation. But it must be appreciated that in those early days, as in prehistoric times, their very outlook did not allow of any separation of what we now consider 'legitimate' observation and induction, from astrology and magic. 'Distillation' of this kind lay far in the future, and the ground had to be prepared before it could take place. In consequence, we shall find the astronomy of the early civilizations interwoven with strands of other studies and superstitions.

The Chinese civilization and its astronomical achievements still require much study. At the present time, however, there does not appear to be any sound evidence to indicate that Chinese astronomy exerted any significant influence on Western developments. Moreover, studies of Chinese records are particularly difficult. This is not only on account of the usual problems of finding scholars with a scientific training who are, at the same time, really familiar with ancient Chinese culture; it is also due to the difficult problem of dating their ancient records (because a completely new system of numbering years began with the accession of each emperor), and to the need for a scholar's critical faculties to be more than usually on the *qui vive* to ensure that he does not read into the past the ideas and concepts from a later age. That the Chinese made astronomical observations is, of course, clear. They constructed sundials, often with the dial inclined to the horizontal, and developed a system of constellations with a 'zodiac' of 28 'houses'. The Sun was, therefore, carefully observed and it would also appear that they knew of the obliquity of the ecliptic as far back as the first millennium B.C. Eclipses were carefully recorded, not only on account of the obviously striking nature of the phenomena, but also because of the religious significance which was attached to such an occurrence. Formal religious observances had to be carried out, and from at least one story of the death of two astronomers who failed in their duty to predict an eclipse one can with some certainty accept the claim that the Chinese knew of some solar-lunar cycle which gave them knowledge of the recurrence of eclipses.

The Moon was also carefully observed as well as the five planets visible to the unaided eye; indeed it is claimed that records dating from 2500 B.C. make mention of a conjunction of all five planets. Comets, solar haloes and other phenomena of a transitory kind were also observed and recorded. However, none of these observations seem to have led to any particular astronomical use of arithmetic or mathematics; even though as far back as the third millennium B.C. a sexagesimal system was in use. While there is no doubt that familiarity with numbers and number relationships was part of the stock-in-trade of the ancient Chinese philosopher, we have here a case, as Sarton[1] says, of coming close to mathematics and then drifting away.

Chinese cosmology seems to have been concerned, primarily, with the Sun, Moon and stars. All three were sacred symbols which only the emperor had the right to wear. The Sun personified heat, action and light, indeed qualities which to those who never conceived of the emancipation of woman, were attributable solely to the male! It was the Moon which they believed to exhibit the 'female qualities' of darkness, coldness, passiveness, trouble and evil. The stars, together with the Sun and Moon, exhibited to the Chinese mind a

[1] Sarton, *A History of Science*, London, 1953, p. 12.

universal harmony. In view, as has already been said, of the cyclic nature of astronomical phenomena, this outlook can not only be appreciated but also commended; after all Man saw in the heavens an apparently eternal creation which he, certainly, had no power to alter by one iota. Overlying this cosmological harmony was the concept of duality. The Sun and Moon, or solar and lunar principles, *Yang* and *Yin*, ruled Chinese philosophy, and were therefore taken to be the ruling forces operating in the universe.

The vast land of India early supported civilized communities. However, virtually nothing has been so far discovered which can give credence to the legendary idea that it is here we must look for the cradle of science. Archæological excavations of the cities of Hindustan have laid bare no evidence of careful and systematic observation. Tables have been found, together with instructions for their computation, but the claim that their basis was a solar-lunar-planetary conjunction in the fourth millennium B.C. is clearly a myth, for calculation has shown that no such conjunction could have occurred; a date for these tables is therefore more than doubtful. The sages of India are traditionally noted for wisdom but what form this took is unknown. It is certainly possible that it was of a primarily religious nature, epitomized in the anecdote by Aristoxenus in his *Lives* that Socrates, who flourished in Athens in the fourth century B.C., was asked by a Hindu sage what, as a philosopher, he studied; on replying that he was concerned with human things the Hindu expressed contempt for, in his opinion, it was divine things which must first be understood before any other knowledge could be assimilated. Perhaps then scholars will look in vain for any influence from India on the early studies of astronomy.

Before we turn to the two civilizations which had so considerable an effect on the Western civilizations which were to develop much later, something must be said of the astronomy of ancient Mexico. Although this appears, at the present time, to have no significance for a historical sketch of the developments leading up to present cosmological speculation in Western civilization, it is of itself interesting and may, conceivably, become of importance as ethnological and related studies progress. The evidence at present available is primarily in the form of carvings, the interpretation of which has been the province of archæologists, although the Maya (Indian) civilization certainly later developed a hieroglyph type of writing.

The main astronomical work of the ancient Mexicans lay in the preparation of calendars and the observation of the Sun, Moon and the planets, with special emphasis on Venus. They are reported to have known of the obliquity of the ecliptic, although it does not seem clear at what date they became aware of this. However, their observations of equinoxes, solstices and meridian altitudes would, of course, provide them with the raw material for such a determination. Their observing tools consisted of a gnomon in the form of a vertical style fixed to the ground, and use was also made of a pair of crossed sticks which were 'lined up' with distant yet recognizable points on the horizon, the crossed sticks being mounted on the top of the pyramidal structure which lay within the walls of their temples. It is also claimed that they observed the heliacal risings and settings of the Sun and, as we have previously pointed out in connexion with prehistoric man, this technique is likely to have been an early development. Constellations were recognized, the Pleiades as the 'rattlesnake' and Gemini as the 'tortoise', the stars Castor and Pollux being used as guides. The apparent rotation of the heavens about the north celestial pole was also known, while it has been claimed that they were aware that the Milky Way was composed of myriads of separate stars. The latter claim would seem rather an hyperbole, for the unaided eye cannot resolve the hazy band into individual sources, although the suggestion that the Mexicans early formed a 'zodiac'[1] of thirteen constellations would appear reasonable, especially in view, as previously mentioned, of their interest in the Sun and, therefore, in heliacal risings and settings. Their interest in the Sun and Moon would of itself have brought an interest in eclipses even if these phenomena had not aroused wonder and speculation of themselves. Except, possibly, for their determination of the obliquity of the ecliptic, the work mentioned above seems to have been carried out in the 'Pre-Classic' era of Mayan civilization which archæologists date as from 1500 B.C. to A.D. 317.

The Mayans concerned themselves much with the calendar, and they had two in use, each for various purposes. The first we may term their agricultural calendar. This was composed of 365 days with an extra day added every fourth year; in fact they knew that the length of the 'tropical year' was not an exact number of days and used the value 365·25.[2] Two forms of division of this agricultural calendar were used. The Mayans took eighteen 'months' of twenty days each, adding five or six intercalary days, while the Nahoan solution was to divide the year into twenty-eight weeks of thirteen days each, and add one or two intercalary days as required.

The second main calendar system was an astronomical one, and consisted of 260 days. The reason for adopting this figure seems likely to have been due to the combination of the number 20, the basis of the vigesimal system which they used for computation, and 13, a number which they believed to have a special significance. But it must also be noted that, as

[1] Zodiac: a word derived from the Greek word ζωδιακός (zōdiakos) meaning *of* or *containing animals* and used to refer to the band of constellations lying near the ecliptic.

[2] It has been claimed that the Mayans actually used the figure of 365·2420 days for the tropical year. The present (1960) value is 365·24219, and so close a correspondence really requires strong confirmation. Noriega (see footnote 1, facing page) does not, however, find such confirmation in his work on the Sun Stone.

Noriega[1] points out, integral multiples of 260 give integral multiples of the synodic periods of the Moon, the planet Mercury, and within a relatively small margin of error, the synodic periods of Venus and Mars.

In view of the great interest which was taken by the Mayans in synodic periods we have here an additional and important reason for the use of the 260-day calendar. In common with other early civilizations they sought long time-scales wherein their computations would be repeated; they made use of the period of 52 years and thus linked both agricultural and astronomical calendars.[2] Moreover, in view of the importance, already mentioned, of the figure 13 the ancient Mexicans must have derived peculiar satisfaction from the satisfactoriness of the 52-year cycle, which is an integral multiple of 13. They also used long periods known as 'anos' or 'years' of particular planets – for example the 'year of Venus' was a period of 584 lunations (i.e. synodic period in days of Venus[3] multiplied by synodic period of the Moon, also in days). Cosmologically the astronomers of ancient Mexico developed what we may term a primarily polytheistic universe. The Sun was worshipped and they held the 'cyclic' belief that several 'worlds' had existed prior to the present one. The heavens were, as with other civilizations, believed to be in the form of a dome which, however, was supported by four gods. Venus was worshipped and in the 'Classic' period (A.D. 317 to 889) a temple was erected to her honour, and the planet's synodic period held a place of particular importance. Early Mexican astronomy stretches back, then, to the second millennium B.C. and shows a careful application to observation assisted by a mathematics which used not only a vigesimal system but

[1] Raul Noriega, *La Piedra del Sol y 16 Monumentos Astronomicos del Mexico Antiguo*, Mexico (privately published), 1954(?).

[2] $365.25 \times 52 = 18{,}993$ days $= 260 \times 73$.

[3] The synodic period was taken as 584 days. This is only approximate. The exact value is 583·92 days and, according to Noriega, even this error was known and allowance made for the approximate value of 584.

also positional digits and a symbol for zero. Inherent in their studies is what we may justly term a 'scientific approach' even if we wish to restrict this compliment to their calendar work only. This development was, however, carried on in comparative isolation; because of this, we shall – regretfully – not have occasion to refer to it again.

The two other civilizations to which we must now turn are those of Egypt and Babylonia. Both, because of their geographical position, had a profound effect on the developments which we shall be tracing in later chapters. The map (page 38) shows the area in which these civilizations flourished as well as the wider Mediterranean area which became such a centre of scientific progress under the 'Greeks'.

We first consider the 'Babylonians', whose influence was certainly important, although it must be appreciated that the extent to which Babylonian astronomy affected the later Greek civilization has still to be fully assessed. At least we can glean only a partially complete picture, due not least to the painstaking and scholarly work of Neugebauer, Kugler and others. The Babylonians have left much material in the form of small baked clay tablets upon which information is inscribed in 'cuneiform' script, so called because writing was carried out using a wedge-shaped tool which gave the characters a deep head and thin tail. Mathematical tablets which Neugebauer has recently examined and discussed[1] date from about 1800 B.C., and display a very high standard of mathematical attainment. Clearly they were preceded by substantial mathematical work during many previous centuries. On the other hand, astronomical texts of the greatest significance date from a late period, namely from about 300 B.C. to the beginning of the Christian era. Although we are here concerned with the astronomical endeavours of the Babylonians it must be appreciated that the term 'Babylonian' is really a generic one.

---

[1] Neugebauer, *The Exact Sciences in Antiquity*, Princeton, London and Copenhagen, 1952.

EARLY CIVILIZATIONS

Archæologists have traced back the history of Mesopotamia ('A' on map) to around 3300 B.C., the date of the earliest writings. The beginnings of the Babylonian civilization lay in the fertile area which lies between the Mediterranean Sea and the Persian Gulf and faces the Syrian desert. The civilization from which the mathematical texts come was preceded by the Sumerians, who flourished between 2500 and 3000 B.C., and who did much to develop the mathematics which reached such a high peak in the second millennium B.C. The Sumerian civilization settled near the mouth of the Euphrates and, in fact, cultivated the land which lay between the Euphrates on the west and the Tigris on the east ('B' on map). They reclaimed the marshes near the Persian Gulf, and considered themselves superior to the mountain dwellers to the north and the nomadic tribes which crossed and re-crossed the Syrian desert. Indeed they believed in the existence of a previous 'golden age' when there was one language and world peace, a conception, no doubt, taken over and modified to a monotheistic pattern by the Hebrews. In the third millennium B.C. the Semitic race which occupied Accad, the area further north of Sumer, conquered the Sumerians, but, as Sarton puts it,[1] 'they' (the Sumerians) 'conquered their conquerors' and their superior culture continued not only to hold its own but also to develop. That it did not lose its identity is perhaps best shown by the fact that subsequent kings styled themselves 'of Sumer and Accad'. The 'Ur of the Chaldees' of the Bible and birthplace of Abraham was a Sumerian city, and it is due to the excavations of Sir Leonard Woolley and others that so much is now known about their civilization. Not later than about 1800 B.C. the Sumerians were brought into contact with the Mediterranean by the Amurru people (the Amorites of the Old Testament), and by 1700 B.C. the great Hammurabi had established the capital at Babylon and become the supreme ruler of the whole of Mesopotamia. So

[1] Sarton, *A History of Science*, London, 1953, p. 60.

came the generically named Babylonian civilization. The Sumerian language remained as a 'classical' language, the Semitic Accadian tongue being the one of everyday use. Wars again followed Hammurabi's rule and the country remained unsettled until the first millennium B.C., when the Assyrian empire consolidated its position. The land next became part of the Persian empire and finally, around 300 B.C., came under the Seleucid domination which was contemporaneous with the 'Hellenistic' culture we shall be considering in the next chapter. The Babylonians modified the Sumerian culture in some ways, as also did the Assyrians, while Egyptian influence (of the 'New Kingdom') also had its effect. In discussing 'Babylonian' astronomy, especially around the fourth century B.C., we are then dealing with a complex of views and ideas which have gone through many vicissitudes.

The 'Babylonians' were competent observers, although they cannot be said to have made any exceptional strides in this department of astronomy. Indeed the Sumerians and their culture developed a qualitative rather than quantitative picture of the universe. They did however recognize the conspicuous constellations, and named the brightest of the fixed stars. Moreover, like the ancient Mexicans, they deified the Sun, Moon and Venus and laid the foundations for 'judicial' astrology, that is to say astrology applied to affairs of state; but in fairness, it must be pointed out that they did not descend to the baser study of personal horoscopes. It is, of course, easy for us to be cynical about even the use of judicial astrology, but we must remember that this was not only a stimulating force behind astronomical observation but also something far preferable to unadulterated magic which would be the only other alternative at this time. Astrology, judicial or otherwise, is concerned with change, and the Sumerians interested themselves in the behaviour of the planets. They observed these at times of special interest, at what they called 'opposition', that is when the planet was rising at sunrise or setting at sunset, and at stationary points. In general, they were concerned with phenomena near the horizon. This preference would, of course, make for difficulties in accurate observation due to the effects of refraction by the Earth's atmosphere.

They used a solar calendar of 360 days and also a lunar calendar. Months of 29 or 30 days were recognized, and these alternated with one another except when necessity demanded a break in the regularity so that the total should reach the required amount. An intercalated month was used to bring the solar and lunar calendars into step, and certainly by 2294 B.C. it was known that these insertions occurred in an eight-year cycle. This Babylonian calendar was the model on which the Hebrew, Greek and early Roman ones were based.

The next stage of development which can be traced with real definitiveness is that of the Assyrian period in texts known as the 'mul apin' which are really a summary of Babylonian astronomical knowledge at that time; it seems likely that they were based on older material. Here we find the fixed stars classified positionally into three bands parallel to the celestial equator, the middle band covering stars within the declination range $\pm 15°$. Movements of the planets and the Moon were observed and records of these are inscribed on the tablets, as also are movements of the Sun observed by means of a gnomon, the results being given in the form of lengths of shadow cast. The tablets also record what, in fact, are various problems of elementary positional astronomy, and although really of a descriptive character the rationalism of the approach is something to be remarked. It is clear that *c.* 700 B.C. court astronomers were employed in order to carry out systematic observations and apply these as omens for astrological use. Eclipses were observed, and Ptolemy (*fl.* A.D. 130) stated that these records were continuous from *c.* 747 B.C. until his day. The Assyrian tablets record, in addition to astronomical phenomena, other happenings which at that time, and indeed for a very long time after, were not differentiated from true astronomical occurrences. Such were solar and lunar haloes, which they seem to have placed on a level with solar and lunar eclipses. Comets were no doubt observed also, though nothing definite regarding them appears in the records; however, unless there were no comets visible to the naked eye for millennia (a state of affairs which is not credible) they must have been noted and recorded for astrological purposes if for no other reason. Perhaps as archæological work on Babylonia continues, such records will come to light.

All this astronomical endeavour had, as we have hinted, a firm mathematics behind it. The Sumerians seem to have had an 'algebraic' cast of mind just as the 'Greeks' had a 'geometrical' one. They worked much with reciprocals, and delighted in abstract mathematical methods, sometimes calculating problems in a needlessly complex manner. They had methods enabling them to measure the areas of rectangles and right-angled isosceles triangles; they knew that the angle formed by the two lines from the ends of the diameter of a circle formed a right-angle when inscribed in a semi-circle. They dealt also with regular solids and had means for computing the volumes of a rectangular parallelepiped, a right circular cylinder, the frustrum of a cone and of a square pyramid. However, their calculation of circular measurements was not as developed as one might expect and, for example, they took 3 as the value for π. Nevertheless, Babylonian mathematics contained some very important concepts. The position factor in numeration, with the use in Seleucid times of a symbol for zero, could have had a very profound effect if it had not become 'lost' and had to wait for introduction into Western Europe until the advent of the 'Arabic' number system. They also extended their numerical scale to submultiples as well as multiples of the unit, and used the same base for computation and measuring but, again, both

EARLY CIVILIZATIONS

these concepts were 'lost' and all that really became passed on was the sexagesimal system of numeration, which they constantly applied to strictly mathematical or astronomical matters.

The latest of the Babylonian astronomical texts come from the Seleucid period. From these Neugebauer[1] has concluded that certainly by *c.* 400 B.C. a systematic mathematical astronomy had been developed. They had in use a lunar calendar to which they applied a rule of 7 intercalations every 19 years, and this presupposes a knowledge that 235 lunar months were equal to 19 solar years. This is typical of the mathematical approach of the Seleucids where x intervals of one kind are equated to y of another kind, and were used for the preparation of ephemerides.[2] Their mathematical methods, as already remarked, were not geometrical but 'algebraic'. Indeed they employed what Neugebauer[3] aptly calls 'linear zig-zag' functions. These linear functions have maximum and minimum values and are separated by a set period of time; in one of their tables, for example, the Seleucids used this method for the computation of an ephemeris for the annual variation in the apparent solar velocity. Ephemerides were also prepared for eclipses, and these gave values for the amount of immersion of the lunar and solar disks into shadow. Moreover, the essentially mathematical approach of these late Babylonian astronomers is shown clearly in the fact that where no immersion occurs, and hence no eclipse, the values are given in a 'negative' form.

During the Seleucid period there was developed the hemicycle, a special kind of sundial which formed the basis of

[1] Neugebauer, op. cit.

[2] 'Ephemerides' [singular: 'ephemeris'] is a term derived from the Greek ἐφήμερος meaning 'lasting only a day'; it is now used exclusively for astronomical tables giving day by day or, at least, calendar dates for the appearances of heavenly bodies.

[3] Neugebauer, op. cit., p. 106.

many later variations. This consisted of a cubical block of stone or wood into which was carved an opening of hemispherical shape. A pointer or style protruded from the body of the block, its end reaching exactly to the centre of the hemisphere. The path traced by the shadow of the end of the style was virtually a circular arc, the exact path depending upon the altitude of the Sun and therefore the season of the year. A number of arc lines were inscribed on the dial and each divided into twelve equal portions or 'hours'. It must be noted that these hours were of the so-called 'temporary' kind, that is to say they themselves varied as between one season of the year and another. The design of the device is attributed to the Berosus (*fl. c.* 300 B.C.) and the ability to develop it was no doubt a result of the high mathematical attainment which was the Babylonian legacy. Hemicycles of various designs were in use as late as the tenth century A.D., for more than a thousand years after the original Babylonian design.

The concept of a zodiac with twelve sections each of 30° was in use, and the basic period relationships between the Moon and the five planets were known. Variations of daylight and night-time were computed for the various seasons, and their calendar system was such that a new 'day' was taken as beginning in the evening. No exclusively observational texts have yet been unearthed, but it is clear that there must have been much careful work of which the ephemerides are evidence, for however excellent their mathematical tools these required the raw material of observation for their application.

Cosmologically the Babylonian picture was a rationalization of their general views, and if not exceptional it was at least free of the mythology which coloured the Egyptian cosmos. A reference to the map ('A,B,C') will show how much the Babylonian civilization depended on the river Euphrates, and how the land on which they found themselves could be considered as surrounded by water on at least three sides.

Small wonder therefore that so rationally minded a civilization should consider the Earth as a flat disk surrounded by water. Towards one end lay a mountain range (identifiable with the Munzer mountains) and the source of the Euphrates. The heavens were believed to be dome-shaped, but unlike the ancient Mexicans the Babylonians did not postulate gods for supporting it, believing that mountains carried out the duty – again an example of their more rational approach. They also believed that the Earth was fixed and that the heavens revolved round it, but we know of nothing about any general ideas they may have had of planetary motion and an explanation for the stationary points of the planets. Nevertheless in Babylonian astronomy, incomplete though our knowledge of it is, we see the development of a rational system of astronomy and cosmology which certainly had an influence on the later Hellenistic civilization, and is a tribute to the genius of the people of the 'two rivers'.

Finally we turn to a brief consideration of Egyptian astronomy, and its background. The Egyptian civilization developed, like the Babylonian, close to a river, and was concentrated around the Nile with an emphasis south of the delta ('D' on the map). The Nile periodically overflowed its banks and thereby irrigated the surrounding land, so helping to produce an abundance of crops. The exact date of the beginning of the Egyptian civilization is unknown; whether it was anterior to the Mesopotamian we do not know. All we can be certain of is that it did not lag far behind or start much earlier. At the time our interest in them begins, the Egyptians had developed many technical arts; they cultivated crops of barley, wheat and flax, wove linen and some time late in the third millennium B.C. they developed writing. Unlike the Sumerians they did not use clay tablets and cuneiform script, and they certainly developed their methods independently. The earliest Egyptian writings that we have come from the 'Old Kingdom' (*c.* 2600–2100 B.C.), and are composed of twenty-four alphabetic signs[1] which later became increased in number. These alphabetic signs were not an alphabet as we now understand it, and were supplemented by a number of more complex symbols or hieroglyphics.[2] Hieroglyphics are easier to read than alphabetical symbols provided, of course, we are familiar with them. Even now they are still in use in certain scientific subjects, viz., astronomical, chemical and mathematical signs. The Egyptians also made an important development in the invention of papyrus. After all, an inexpensive and convenient material to write upon is vital if anything of any extensive kind is to be kept unless it be special records which can always be inscribed on stone. Papyrus was derived from the pith of the stem of the tall sedge (*Cyperus papyrus*) which grew in abundance among the marshes of the Delta. Its fabrication was simple and the material was widely used, so widely in fact that at the beginning of the Christian era the emperor Tiberius had to legislate for its rationing! The material was made into rolls composed of sheets glued together end to end; and sizes varied from about 3 inches to nearly 19, and were often of great length, over a hundred feet not being unusual. Many texts have therefore been found in their entirety, protected by the extremely dry Egyptian climate. The date of the invention of papyrus is uncertain, but seems to have been some time in the second century B.C.

Egyptian astronomy, like Babylonian, began in the earliest times; the climate was inviting. However, the Egyptians seem to have had a more religious (or should one say 'mythological'?) cast of mind than the Sumerians, they early considered the heavens from this point of view, and it was near the beginnings of their civilization that the goddess Nut was conceived. Her body was believed to encircle the heavens the

---

[1] An interesting table of these is given in Sarton, op. cit., p. 21.
[2] From the Greek ἱερός (hieros) = sacred and γλύφω (glupho) an engraving tool.

EARLY CIVILIZATIONS

while she supported herself, somewhat ignominiously, upon hands and feet. Perhaps it was because of this concept of a deity so large as to cover the entire heavens that the Egyptian constellations were of immense size, being composed of much larger groups of stars than we are accustomed to use; for example the constellation Nekht took almost six hours to cross the meridian. In plotting their constellations the Egyptians developed an unique concept which had considerable influence for many centuries in the fields of astrology and alchemy; this was the 'decan'. The decans were groups of stars (not constellations) so arranged that the first star of each decan was seen to rise after sunset ten days later than the first star of the previous decan – in other words the decans were areas of the sky some 10° across. The idea was of no special importance in mathematical astronomy but was used as a means of indicating time during the night.

As has been mentioned, the annual flooding of the Nile was an event of the greatest significance. It occurred in July, and although not regular to the day, it coincided closely enough with the heliacal rising of Sirius. To the Egyptians Sirius was known as Sothis, and because of this their astronomical calendar contained 365·25 days. The civil calendar contained, however, only 365 days. Originally, in company with every other ancient civilization, the Egyptians had made use of a lunar calendar. However, the Nile flooding had, early on, shown the impracticability of a calendar based on anything which was not directly dependent upon the seasons, and before any establishment of religious festivals had become wedded to a lunar computation, solar calendars became adopted. Very wisely they divided their civil calendar of 365 days into twelve months each of thirty days, and then added a holiday season of five intercalary days. Every four years the heliacal rising of Sothis became one day removed from the astronomical calendar, and this gave rise to the Sothic cycle, which was the period of time when the astronomical calendars and the heliacal risings came again into step. It was, as the Egyptians clearly recognized, a total of 1,460 years ($= 4 \times 365$).

Egyptian mathematics was very different in essence from Sumerian or later Babylonian. The Egyptian outlook can be claimed to have had an entirely practical bias. Problems concerning areas or volumes were merely an extension of numerical methods; no generalizations were made, thus their astronomy for ever remained at a low level of development and never reached the mathematical level of the Babylonian or the Greek. The Egyptians devised no planetary hypothesis, either simple or complex, descriptive or ingenious, nor do they appear to have concerned themselves with solar or lunar eclipses – no detailed observations have come down to us, and even Ptolemy, who made it his job to delve into early records, found nothing.

The Egyptians, with their practical cast of mind, were concerned with time determination, and so developed various types of sundial. The well-known merkhet was purely a plumb line which cast a vertical or horizontal shadow (depending on the surface near to it) but by the eighth century B.C. the cross-staff type had appeared. Sundials of this type varied in minor details but, in essence, the device consisted of a straight base to which a perpendicular cross-piece was attached at one end; the base was placed in a direction with its axis due east–west and the shadow of the cross-piece fell on to gradations inscribed on the base. Such a sundial had to be reversed at noon, the cross-piece lying to the east in the morning and to the west in the afternoon. Later the base was extended so that the cross-piece lay across its centre, and thus the need for reversing the dial at noon was obviated. As with the Babylonians, the hours inscribed varied in duration according to season.

Cosmologically the Egyptians did not develop what we would call a scientific scheme. Their ideas were not on the same level as the Babylonian, and we can perhaps best term it a polytheistic mélange, but in doing so we must remember we are expressing a judgement made from our knowledge of developments subsequent to the Egyptian civilization and with the rational mechanistic approach of modern science in mind. We can claim that this criticism is valid provided we realize that the ancient Egyptians would have profoundly disagreed – and from their point of view, with good reason. Their scheme supposed a flat Earth and an arc of stars, but here any similarity with the Babylonian picture ended for, as we have already mentioned, the arc of the heavens was the body of the sky goddess Nut and the Earth the body of the Earth god Qed. The motion of the Sun was simply explained – every day Nut gave birth to the Sun which travelled over her body. She also gave birth at night to the stars, although in a later picture the sun-god's death sentence every sunset was repealed and he was allowed to continue his journey through the land of the dead so that he appeared in the east each dawn. The god of the air, Slu, was depicted as helping to support Nut's body. That the sun-god travelled in a barge over the body of Nut is, no doubt, an indication that in Egypt as well as in Babylonia the idea was held that there was water above the starry dome and this was, of course, natural enough as a primitive conception, for rain was observed to fall from the sky. The planets were also believed to travel in barges and it was noticed that, on occasions, Mars (which has a very marked retrograde motion) sailed backwards. Neugebauer[1] sums up the Egyptian contribution to astronomical science by referring to their '. . . crude observational schemes, partly religious, partly practical in purpose' and then goes on to say 'Ancient science was the product of very few men; and these few happened not to be Egyptians'. We must agree, but nevertheless remember that they had a culture which was well developed artistically and administratively, and that they

[1] Neugebauer, op. cit., p. 86.

were excellent engineers. If we do this we shall begin to see how the general outlook of a nation or a civilization can be scientifically blind and how, if this is so, their culture is incomplete and their contribution and effect on other civilizations and nations is less powerful than it might otherwise have been.

Chapter 3

GREEK IDEAS – FIRST PHASE

Of all early civilizations, the Greek has had the most profound and lasting effect on the science of Western Europe. This is due not only to the genius of the Greek mind in matters of natural philosophy, but also to many circumstances attending its transmission in later centuries to Western scholars. We shall briefly trace this transmission of Greek scientific culture in a later chapter, but before doing so must try to get clear what views were held, something of the attitude of mind which conditioned them, and also some brief idea of the environment in which this great scientific tradition grew up.

The earliest Greek civilization was centred on the island of Crete ('E' on map). This, now known as the Minoan, was independent of the Babylonian and the Egyptian cultures and its beginnings have been traced back to c. 3000 B.C. It spread, as time went on, over the whole Mediterranean area due, primarily, to the fact that the Cretans early established themselves as a seafaring power. The Minoan civilization reached the peak of its development about 1600 B.C. It then came under the Mycenæans for about three centuries, after which there followed a series of invasions. These appear to have taken place in three main waves.

The first was an invasion of Thessaly ('F' on map) from the west, the people from Thessaly moving to Bœotia ('G' on map); the second, the Dorian invasion from the north which overran the Peloponnesus and the Minoans and Mycenæans at Crete. Thirdly the north-western people migrated from Epiros ('H' on map) either to Apulia or the gulf of Corinth and the north-west of the Peloponnesus ('J' on the map).

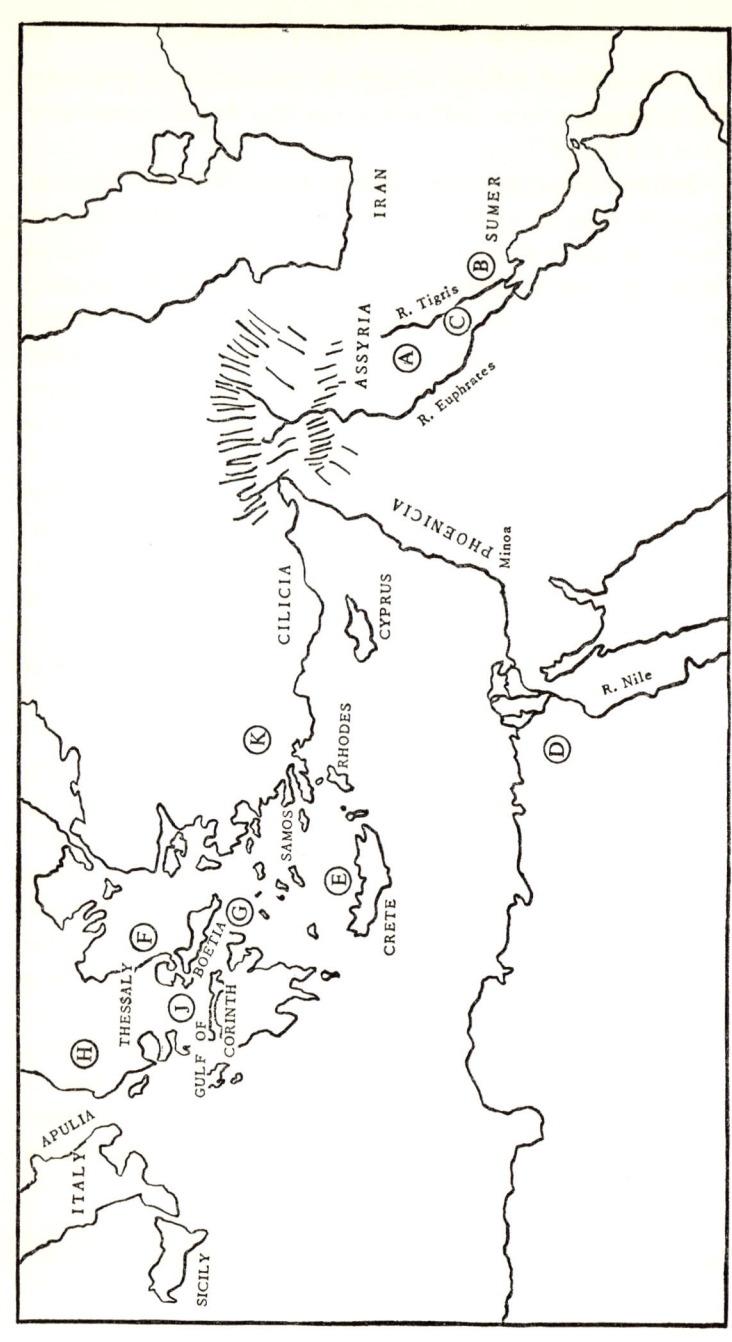

It is difficult and, indeed, it might be misleading, to give dates for these migrations; suffice it to say that they occurred soon after the fall of Troy.

Before discussing early Greek astronomy brief mention must be made of the Phœnicians. They became established on the coast north of Palestine, spoke a Semitic tongue and by 1580 B.C. were a great trading power, their ships certainly travelling as far west as Spain. They made the vital cultural step, never reached by the Egyptians, of developing an alphabet. This alphabet contained no short vowels, but made exclusive use of syllabic symbols and was, perhaps, a result of need forced on them by their international trading; it is delightfully described by Sarton[1] as a 'masterpiece of international brokerage'. Alphabets of a similar kind, but developed later, were the Hebrew and the Arabic. The Greeks, of course, developed the concept and provided symbols for all vowels, both long and short. We can then credit the Phœnicians with the first true alphabet,[2] and certainly it had a profound effect in the dissemination of information, and as a tool for expression and meditation by the philosopher.

The main influence on early Greek astronomy was Egyptian, while it was the Babylonians who affected later ideas. Yet the Babylonian calendar would have accompanied their traders just as the Egyptian calendar was the travelling companion of Egyptian merchants. Perhaps, therefore, it was in this way that the Greeks early adopted a long time-scale, the Saros, which was originally of 3,600 years' duration. They recognized their own constellations and did not use the immense constructions of the Egyptians; the Pleiades, the Hyades, Orion, Ursa Major and Boötes were known, and heliacal risings and settings observed. But the very earliest true Greek contribution to astronomy, that found in Homer and Hesiod,

---

[1] Sarton, op. cit., p. 109.
[2] The Ugaritic alphabet, discovered by Schaeffer at Rās Shamrā, may be older. It follows the same order of letters as the Phœnician.

was primarily a cosmology. Yet it was a cosmology with a difference. From the beginning the Greek approach showed what would seem to be the genius for a geometrical and symmetrical approach. The universe as a whole was conceived of as spherical in shape! The Earth was taken as flat and floating on water, the primeval substance; the latter was in all probability a legacy from Egypt, where after the inundation of the Nile the shoots of living plants were seen and which, therefore, gave every excuse for such a concept. The stars were, clearly, affixed to a dome, and Hades, the abode of the dead, was thought of as lying below the Earth at *an equal distance* from the heavens above. This gave a spherical shape to the universe, and it is this idea of *equal distance* which is striking and so significant. It is a product of the Homeric period, which is generally notable not for its science – there was little – but as an age of literary genius, of decorative beauty and practical arts for living more elegantly. This age lasted but a few centuries (*c*. 900–700 B.C.).

The next great stage came in the sixth century with Ionian developments. These occurred on the west coast of Asia Minor ('K' on the map). An early tradition that Egypt was the cradle of science and learning had grown up; the first natural philosopher of whom we have any knowledge (and that is from the writings of others) is Thales (*c*. 624–548? B.C.). He came from Miletus, one of the twelve cities of Ionia, and a great trading port with good surrounding fruit-growing and agricultural land. There were a number of Milesian colonies along the shores of the Sea of Marmara and the Black Sea, and one in the Nile delta. The Ionians, like the Cretans, were naturally inquisitive and curious; and with the ever-changing interest which surrounds a great seaport, the stimulation of the philosophically minded may easily be imagined. Thales is reputed to have visited Egypt, and no doubt it was to Naucratis, the colony on the Nile delta, that he went. He was a man of great practical abilities, and was one of the seven wise men of the Ionian tradition;[1] indeed there are a number of legends concerning him. An oft-repeated one of these[2] is that at a battle in 585 B.C. between the Lydians and Persians, a solar eclipse occurred and fighting ceased. Thales is reputed to have predicted this, and have been proclaimed two years later as a 'wise man' by the oracle of Delphi. Another story, told by Aristotle, is that Thales predicted (meteorologically) a great olive harvest and thereupon gave deposits for the use of all the olive-presses in Miletus and Chios. At the time he did this (winter) there were no bids against him, and he secured his monopoly without much capital outlay. When harvest came, many presses were suddenly wanted; Thales let them out on his own terms and so accumulated considerable wealth. Scientifically Thales laid the foundations for the Ionians of astronomy and geometry. From Egypt he brought back some rudimentary knowledge about the recurrence of eclipses, and many geometrical facts which he began to synthesize into geometrical principles. In his astronomy he extended the concept of the primeval nature of water, and claimed that it was the basic substance out of which the world was made. This was certainly a rational view. Water was found in many forms and in every place, and its obvious connexion in the Nile valley with living things has already been mentioned. Clearly Thales was seeking a synthesis in the field of cosmology just as he sought one in geometry. He still held that the Earth was flat and that it floated on water. He propounded also the Homerian concept of a spherical universe. In this Thales seems to have been concerned not with placing Hades at a distance below the Earth equal to that of the heavens above, but to obtain a scheme which was both geometrically balanced and in accordance with observation. We can, with some cause, claim that his approach was rationalistic.

[1] Another was Solon of Athens, the great lawgiver.
[2] For fuller details see Sarton, op. cit., p. 170.

Contemporaneous with Thales, although then spoken of as his 'disciple', was Anaximander, also of Miletus. To him the primeval substance was not water, but some substance as yet unknown and indeterminate. He therefore kept the idea of a unity in creation but refused to commit himself as to the nature of the basic material. Anaximander used a gnomon for observing the shadows cast by the Sun at different times of the year, and it is likely that Thales also used this device, which seems to have been known from great antiquity. However, the interpretation of the results of the use of a gnomon will depend upon the concept held of the shape of the Earth. To both Thales and Anaximander the Earth was flat, although the latter believed that the thickness of the terrestrial disk was one-third of its diameter, and this, of course, prevented anything in the nature of latitude being appreciated. He speculated on the distance and sizes of the heavenly bodies. The Sun he believed to be a ring 28 times the size of the Earth in diameter, the Moon one of 19 diameters of the Earth. Both, he claimed, were self-luminous, each being seen by light escaping through an aperture in its rim, eclipses occurring when these apertures were temporarily stopped up; partial stoppages accounted for the phases of the Moon. To Anaximander the place of heavy things like rocks and earth lay as low as possible, that is, presumably, to the lower side of the Earth's disk. Lighter substances, water for example, would remain on the upper surface of the Earth while very light 'materials' like air and fire would rise above the Earth. Here then we see the first appearance of the concept of 'natural places' for material substances which was to play so important a part in the physics of later Greek thought. Space was, to Anaximander, truly spherical. In this slowly developing cosmology the Ionian genius for abstract thought based upon their general observations is again clearly to be seen.

The idea, later so much a fixture in the mind of philosophers for many centuries, that the stars were fixed to the inside walls of the spherically-shaped universe which itself rotated, was propounded by Anaximenes (*d*. 528–525 B.C.), a younger contemporary of Anaximander and Thales and, like them, a citizen of Miletus. Anaximenes followed Thales in seeking a primal substance which could be identified with one of the elements found round him, and he eschewed the more abstruse concept of indeterminate material of Anaximander. It is clear that Anaximenes pondered long and deeply on the matter. He concluded that there was more likelihood that air rather than water was the primal substance. Air *was* everywhere, it was necessary for life, and, indeed, it was the very breath of life. It could be felt and yet, at the same time, was intangible. By such considerations as these was Anaximenes led to his concept of air (pneuma) which took on various aspects either by condensation or rarefaction, and he even carried out some observations which led him to conclude that such changes were associated with changes in temperature. Moreover, he likened the organism man, whose breath was the breath of life, with the macrocosm of the world of which the living principle was pneuma – and this idea of two worlds, micro- and macro-scopic, pervaded much of mediæval thought.

Thales is reputed to have died on the island of Tenedos, which lay about 200 miles north of Miletus. If this is so his views were directly taught here, if not by Thales himself then probably by a 'disciple', which might well have given rise to the tradition of his death having taken place on the island. Whichever alternative may be true, the fact remains that Cleostratus, who certainly lived on the island and was probably born there, imbibed the Miletian teaching. Cleostratus took the obliquity of the ecliptic as something previously determined, possibly either by Thales or by Anaximander. As we have already remarked certainly the latter, and probably both, used a gnomon which, even with the concept of a flat Earth, would be likely to have led to a determination of this quantity. The contribution of Cleostratus himself was that by his own observations he tried to determine the exact times of solstices, and also concerned himself with the zodiacal signs. The zodiac itself had certainly been recognized previously by the Babylonians, but the contribution of Cleostratus was to determine when and among which of the zodiacal constellations the Sun, Moon and planets travelled during the year and to divide these constellations into 'signs' – these may have been purely constellation groups or divisions of 30° each, and it is uncertain whether Cleostratus actually concerned himself with but two signs or with all. No matter; he began such an approach to the problems of planetary motion. He is also attributed with introducing an eight-year cycle of intercalations, which period[1] includes an exact number of days, months and lunations. He may have inherited this from the Babylonians; but whether he did or not, he certainly made use of it in calendar calculations and was responsible for introducing it into Greek astronomy. Cleostratus provided no new general picture of the universe, but what he did in the way of observation and calculation was grist to the cosmological mill of those who followed later.

Ephesus, some 30 miles north of Miletus, was the most famous of the Ionian cities, primarily because of the great temple of Artemis which was built there. Here Heracleitus was born and flourished during the fifth century B.C. He was, by nature, a pessimist and he believed that, because of the transitory nature of all things, only the underlying and invisible harmony which lay below the surface was what mattered. Heracleitus sought the primal and permanent substance but, differing from Thales, Anaximander and Anaximenes, he proposed fire as his solution. Fire was certainly an excellent substance with which to symbolize change and to fit in with his concept of continual up and down motion which

[1] 8 years = 8 × 365·25 = 2922 days = 99 lunations.

constituted change. The rest of Heracleitus' cosmology was a kind of meteorological theory, for he explained the existence of the Sun, Moon and planets as exhalations. Moist exhalations, collected in what is virtually a basin, are ignited as this basin rises from the sea and extinguished as it sets; the fiery basin is what we call the Sun. It shines brightly because it moves high up in very pure air, while the Moon, being lower, moves through denser air and so shines less brightly. These basins sometimes turn, and when this happens we observe eclipses and, presumably, the Moon's phases. The seasons depended, he taught, on particular combinations of bright and dark, and hot and cold, exhalations, while he believed that the Sun was small in size, about the size of a human foot.

Empedocles, who flourished about 450 B.C., came from Agrigentum in Sicily, and was a protagonist of views quainter even than those of Heracleitus. He proposed four elements – earth, air, fire and water – as was done by Pythagoras and his followers, as we shall describe below. But to the four elements Empedocles added two opposing principles, love and hate. These six 'quantities' were eternal and were used to explain the changes observed in all things. He believed that the heavens were composed of crystalline material which was, in essence, condensed air. To this the stars were fixed, and the whole sphere was, he suggested, in rotation. Moreover, he taught that this sphere was half dark and half light, and that as it rotated it gave rise to day and night. Empedocles proposed, no doubt to fit in with this concept, that the Sun was a focal point of reflected fiery light which emanated from a fiery sphere which lay outside the half-dark half-light crystalline one. He was however aware that solar eclipses were due to the Moon passing in front of the Sun (or rather, of the reflections of which it is formed) and he believed that the Moon was distant from the Earth by an amount equal to one-third of the radius of the crystalline sphere. The dual qualities of love and hate might lead us to assume that Empedocles was a religious philosopher, and we should be correct. He was a missionary, and on his journeys sang verses of his own composition, healing sickness and ministering to the religious needs of his fellows – he is even credited with having brought a woman of Agrigentum back to life. In spite of the quaintness of his cosmological speculations he concerned himself with a famous experiment with a clepsydra[1] and with it proved that air had 'substance' – he did this by taking a clepsydra and plunging it in water, the while observing that if he kept his fingers over the orifice at the top water could not enter through the tiny orifices at the bottom. He wrote on rays of light and the process of seeing and also considered that light rays travelled at a finite speed.

Both Heraclitus and Empedocles propounded cosmological ideas which were far from reality and seem, on the face of it, to be a falling-away from the scientific approach which the early Greek natural philosophers appear to have followed. However, the real trouble would seem to be not specially due to any shortcomings of either – we cannot condemn a pessimist for being a pessimist, nor can we claim that his science will *ipso facto* be inferior to that of an optimist; we cannot condemn as without scientific understanding a man who could experiment as Empedocles did with the clepsydra. No; the reason would seem to be due more to the fact that both tried to explain in detail too many phenomena considering the scanty nature of the observational material which they possessed.

The Ionian philosopher was, however, bold in his attacks on the problems which intrigued him and no all-embracing conception was too wide to be considered. Anaxagoras of

---

[1] Clepsydræ were probably known both in Babylon and Egypt and were no doubt in use by the Greeks before the time of Empedocles. However, his experiment using such a device is the first mention occurring in Greek literature.

Clazomenæ[1] was no exception, but he seemed to have more of what we should call the 'scientific approach' than some of his contemporaries. He probably went to Ephesus in his youth, and later certainly moved to Athens, being the first Ionian philosopher to establish himself there. He became a friend of Pericles, who was the most powerful man in the city, but whose standing nevertheless became enhanced by this friendship. However, Pericles, like all great statesmen, had his political enemies. When, at the beginning of the Peloponnesian War, Pericles lost his popularity Anaxagoras also suffered attack and, being convicted of impiety, was banished from the city; he ended his days teaching at Lamsacos in the Dardanelles. Anaxagoras considered problems of general cosmology and physics. He believed that rather than explain change as a 'coming into being' or 'ceasing to be', it was preferable to postulate a chaos of innumerable seeds to which mind gives order. These seeds were not elements but by their mixture and decomposition all changeable phenomena could be explained. Mind gave order to the seeds by causing a general rotation which, in its turn, caused a separation of the seeds into æther and air. Thus we have here the first form of a vortex theory, and the whole concept was one of universal homogeneity. Anaxagoras believed in a flat Earth but realized that the Moon shone by reflecting the light of the Sun. Moreover, he appreciated that eclipses were due to the interposition of the Moon between the Earth and the Sun, and he also put forward the idea that the surface of the Moon was similar to that of the Earth with plains and ravines; however, the Sun, he thought, was just rather larger than the Peloponnesus and was composed of red-hot iron. His ideas of the Sun's composition were, no doubt, coloured by the fall of a large meteorite at Ægos Potamoi, which lay on the northern shore of the Dardanelles. This much interested

[1] Clazomenæ lay some 70 miles N.N.W. of Miletus and 20 miles west of Smyrna.

Anaxagoras, who believed that the object had fallen from the Sun. More than this, Anaxagoras adopted an order for the Sun, Moon and planets which was later universally adopted by Greek astronomers. The stars he thought were stony lumps of material torn from the Earth, and kept in their places by the rotation of the æther, which also kept them luminous. Like Anaximenes he thought of the Earth as floating on air, but he also suggested a physical mechanism for the inclination of north celestial pole which, of course, had been recognized for some time. This explanation was based on the idea of a flat Earth, and Anaxagoras postulated that the Earth's disk tilted downwards at its southern and warmer edge. He correctly explained the Moon's phases and must, therefore, have assumed the Moon to be spherically shaped. The Milky Way he believed to lie in the shadow cast by the Earth, thus permitting us to see more stars because the Sun's light was thereby cut out. If this explanation were correct, then the position of the Milky Way should alter among the fixed stars during the course of the year, but at least it shows that Anaxagoras recognized that the hazy light was made up of separate stars, although his explanation is not the correct one – a classic example of a philosopher obtaining the correct answer using an invalid hypothesis.

We must now turn from the Ionian mainland, and consider the great work carried out in the school of Pythagoras. No attempt will be made to try and differentiate to any great degree between the efforts of Pythagoras himself and his 'disciples' – much that was later developed was credited to the Master, and our concern is with the attitude of mind exhibited, the results obtained and the school's influence on later generations. The biographies of Pythagoras were prepared long after his death, and are full of many tales and legends, yet we know that Pythagoras was born on the island of Samos which lies off the Ionian coast, and that he flourished *c.* 532 B.C. Samos was at this time ruled by Polycrates, a

GREEK IDEAS – FIRST PHASE

tyrant who became extremely rich; some claim that Pythagoras was driven away either by the tyranny he and others had to suffer, or else because of his fear of a Persian invasion. Pythagoras probably visited Egypt, went on to Babylon and then returned to Samos. Soon, however, he wandered abroad again and finally settled in Croton in southern Italy, where he established his philosophical school. He was driven out towards the end of his life, and died at nearby Metapontion c. 497 B.C. Pythagoras was a religious teacher as well as a natural philosopher of great ability, and Russell,[1] for instance, in his inimitable way, has likened him to 'a combination of Einstein and Mrs Eddy'. Pythagoras initiated what may be called a religious order which required an ascetic discipline of its members and abstention from certain foods of which meat and fish, beans and wine were the main items; members of the order, both men and women, wore distinctive garments, went barefoot, and lived in simple fashion and held all things in common. Their doctrines were held under a bond of secrecy. Pythagoras taught the doctrine of transmigration of souls, and regarded life as an exile which was closed by death. After the death of Pythagoras some of his followers were persecuted and some massacred.

Pythagoras had a very strongly mathematical cast of mind, and developed a number mysticism which penetrated even his cosmological speculations. First he differentiated between odd and even numbers, and appreciated that the latter were divisible into two equal parts. Secondly he used dots drawn into patterns on the sand and was thus able to find a number which could 'fill' a certain space. He discovered, for example, that the numbers 1, 3, 6, 10, ... are 'triangular' (. ∴ ∴·) and that the series 1, 4, 9, 16, ... are 'square' (.. ∷ ∷·) Pythagoras was also particularly interested in the fourth of

---

[1] Russell, *History of Western Philosophy*, London, 1946, p. 49.

the triangular numbers because each side of the triangle contained four dots while the rows of dots, counting from top to bottom, were 1, 2, 3 and 4 and these added up to 10. It was also noted that with the square numbers, in order to pass from one square number to the next, one adds dots to two adjacent sides and that the number of dots so added are always odd in number. For example to pass from . to : : three dots are added, to pass from : : to ⋮⋮ the total added is 5, and so on. Hence the rule was developed that the appropriate odd number added to a square number makes another square. Moreover, by adding in succession successive odd numbers to the first square number 1, one obtains a series of squares, thus: $3 + 1 = 4 = 2^2$, $5 + 4 = 9 = 3^2$, $7 + 9 = 16 = 4^2$ ... This is elegant, and one can readily imagine the deep pleasure the Pythagoreans must have experienced at this discovery of pure numbers. Yet it must be appreciated that this discovery was actually made using 'dots', or at least pebbles, for no numerals were available at this early stage of development. Thus was laid the foundations of what we may term the theory of numbers.

Geometrically Pythagoras and his followers made many discoveries, and these discoveries were generalizations on geometrical shapes. The Pythagoreans thus began the 'art' of geometry. They knew that the interior angles of any plane triangle added up to 180°, and of course the famous Theorem of Pythagoras which generalized the ratio of the sides of any plane right-angled triangle also *proved* that this generalization always held true. Indeed it was their ability to prove their generalizations which was so important.

Astronomically it was Pythagoras and his immediate followers who first suggested that the Earth is spherical in shape. This was a break with the Ionian, Babylonian and Egyptian traditions, and a step forward which affected all later astronomy. It may well be that after his many travels Pythagoras, either from his own experience or by talking to sailors, had become aware of certain phenomena such as the apparent sinking of a ship as it passed over the horizon and realized that this would be inexplicable on the basis of a flat Earth; but whatever observations led to doubting the hypothesis of flatness, it was the sphere which was suggested as the most suitable shape – no doubt because the heavens were spherical in shape and such a unifying abstraction would appeal to the type of mind which could delight in the kind of mathematics we have already described. All other heavenly bodies were also held to be of spherical shape, but the astronomical contribution of the Pythagoreans to later developments had other important aspects. The whole concept of uniform circular motions came from them, and although this idea acted as a brake on the development of knowledge until attacked and one might almost say 'conquered' by Kepler in the seventeenth century, it was at the time a great step forward and allowed of an analysis of planetary motions to be made in later centuries. The Pythagoreans suggested that the total circular motion was compounded of two kinds, one a motion from east to west in the plane of the equator every twenty-four hours, and the other a motion from west to east in the plane of the ecliptic. This worked well for the Sun but was less satisfactory for the Moon and the five planets. Pythagoras or his immediate followers also put the spherical Earth at the centre of the universe and believed it to be immovable. Moreover they concerned themselves with the question of the distances of the planets from the Earth. This was linked up with their doctrine that number was the basis of all things, and was a new conception of celestial harmony. Pythagoras had experimented with stringed instruments and had discovered the numerical relationships between the length of a vibrating section and the notes of the musical scale, and especially that the lengths which were in the ratios 12 : 6, 12 : 8 and 8 : 6 gave the intervals we know as the octave, the fifth and the fourth; and while he, like others, was aware of the concept of arithmetic and geometric means, it seems that we must credit him with the idea of harmonic means. The numbers 12, 8 and 6 mentioned above are in harmonic relationship to one another, and this concept of harmonious sounds and number relationships was applied to the positions of the heavenly bodies so that the radii of the circles on which they travelled were believed to be in harmonious proportion to one another. So the idea of the 'music of the spheres' was born. Because of man's gross nature he could not hear these sounds, although some later claimed that Pythagoras himself could do so! When all is said and done Pythagoras was clearly both a pure and an applied mathematician as well as a mystic, and the teachings of his school exerted a profound influence.

A well-known member of this school was Philolaus of Croton, who flourished around 450 B.C. and was, therefore, a contemporary of Socrates. Philolaus probably had much to do with some of the Pythagorean cosmological doctrines we have just discussed, but he is best remembered for his own unique cosmological system. He did not, as some have claimed, propose a heliocentric view, but suggested that in the centre of the spherical universe lay a central fire around which the Earth, Sun, Moon and planets travelled in circular paths. But this was not all. The orbit of the Earth was supposed to lie in the plane of its equator which, of course, helped to explain why no one had ever seen the central fire. Neither the Earth nor the Moon were believed to rotate on their axes, while Greece and the Mediterranean were claimed to lie on that side of the Earth always turned away from the central fire. Moreover, Philolaus proposed another planet which was supposed to travel in a circular orbit lying between the central fire and that of the Earth. This extra planet known as the antichthon or counter-earth performed three duties. First, its motion was such that it lay permanently between the Earth and the celestial fire; secondly it could help to account for eclipses, especially those occurring near the horizon; and thirdly, it made the number of bodies in the universe total ten,[1] a number which had great significance for all Pythagoreans. In this scheme of Philolaus' the orbital path of the Earth round the central fire was believed to take 24 hours, and thus the apparent rotation of the stars was accounted for without having to transfer to them any motion whatsoever. Perhaps it was this which led some to suppose that the system was a heliocentric one, whereas, of course, it was nothing of the kind. It did, however, postulate a moving and, what was then equally important, a spherically-shaped Earth. Later developments of physics brought forth sound arguments against the moving Earth, which as proposed by Philolaus did not of course account for the observed retrograde motions and stationary points in the paths of the five planets.

Finally we must look at the ideas of Leucippus and Democritus, who, in the fifth century, proposed the first atomic theory. But in considering this it must be appreciated that it was a very different theory from that put forward by Dalton in the nineteenth century of our era and developed with such startling and profound results in the twentieth. Leucippus flourished about the middle of the fifth century B.C. and his birthplace is uncertain although various lines of approach make Miletus the most plausible. Democritus developed the idea of Leucippus. Democritus was born in Abdera in Thrace, on the Greek mainland, and carried out his work on the atomic theory about 420 B.C. In his early years Democritus travelled to Babylon, Persia and possibly as far as India. He was in search of knowledge and no doubt learned much on his travels. However, the claim that the atomic theory was something which he brought back with him from the East is so unlikely that we can discredit it.

The kernel of the Leucippian-Democritan atomic theory

---

[1] Saturn, Jupiter, Mars, Mercury, Venus, Sun, Moon, Earth, the counter-earth and the central fire.

was the idea of stability of basic material substance and the reality of motion. The world was believed to be made of two parts, matter and void. Matter consisted of innumerable small particles or atoms, which were solid and could not be further divided. Different substances had atoms of different shapes and sizes and of different 'subtilities' or densities. As the number of atoms was postulated as infinite there was, in theory at any rate, an infinite number of possible substances. The endless change observed to occur in the world is due to the changing conglomerations of the atoms themselves. Democritus did not divorce soul and body, but believed that the soul was composed of the airiest kind of all atoms, while others made up dreams, images and phantoms. Such atoms (psyche) were everywhere, and hence the whole universe was animated. Thus all phenomena of legend, hearsay or experience could be accounted for on the atomic hypothesis. The cosmological views of these atomists were nothing if not ingenious. The atoms were believed to have a tendency permanently to fall, and also to fall with velocities dependent upon their size, the larger pushing aside the smaller so that as a result the whole system undertook a kind of vortex motion. It was believed that the Earth was formed by such vortex action, and that other atoms formed the air and fire which extended to the heavens. Some of these caused vortices also and these became stars and planets. Leucippus returned to the flat Earth theory. He thought that the world was drum-shaped – flat on the surface and slightly raised around the rim. Democritus conceived of the Earth as flat and shaped like a discus, lower at the circumference and higher in the centre, the Earth itself fitting like a lid over the compressed air in the spherical part of the heavens below it. Both believed that the Earth was tilted, being heavier in the north than in the south. The position of the celestial pole was thus accounted for in a way similar to that of Anaxagoras. Leucippus was of the opinion that the Sun was more distant than the other planets, which lay between it and the Moon. Democritus placed the Moon and the morning star nearest to the Earth; the Sun followed next, then came the planets and finally the stars. Democritus, like Anaxagoras, believed the Moon to be a solid body with mountains and plains, and he also believed the Milky Way to be a great concourse of stars.

The atomic theory was a bold attempt to rationalize things as they appeared to be. It was, as we have seen, one of many such attempts to evolve an all-embracing cosmology. Some of these attempts may, at a distance of two thousand five hundred years, seem either jejune or at best based on the wrong premises. Yet we cannot but help looking back with the twentieth-century attitude of mind which is ingrained in us, and should beware of condemning the sincere efforts of others because they had not our present knowledge. Yet if we look with sympathy upon the struggles of the Greeks of the fifth and sixth centuries B.C. we shall see much to admire, and realize that they provided three great corner-stones on which later generations could build. First they conceived of the universe as of spherical shape. This was not due to observation alone – if it had been they could only, like the Babylonians, have supposed it to be hemispherical. But they brought to bear ideas of logic, of symmetry and much imagination. Secondly they finally produced, through Philolaus, the concept of a spherical Earth, and this was so firmly embedded in the philosophic thought which followed that there was no return to a flat Earth hypothesis. Thirdly they took a rational and mechanistic approach to the questions they tried to solve. This may have been, and at most times was, coloured to a greater or lesser extent by religious or æsthetic considerations. But the form of approach was established in principle, and continued to be applied. As we continue our brief sketch of the views of those who flourished during the next four hundred or so years we shall see some of the fruits to which this approach gave birth.

Chapter 4

GREEK IDEAS – SECOND PHASE[1]

It will be convenient to begin our bird's-eye view of what we may term the second phase of Greek astronomy with a brief consideration of the times in which the cosmological views of Plato were formulated. Plato was born about 428 B.C. in Athens; his parents were aristocrats, and he received as good an education as money could buy. When about twenty years of age he met Socrates, and studied under him for eight years. In 404 B.C. Athens had surrendered to the victorious Spartans and the Peloponnesian Wars which had been waged from 431 to 421 and again from 414 to 404 were over. The Spartans were hated, and their supremacy lasted for only a little over 30 years. Athens gave birth to well-to-do bankers, merchants and landowners, but more trouble lay ahead; there were uprisings against the Spartan domination, and in due course Greek independence was lost and the area of Attica came under the Macedonians. Plato was thus born in troublous times, and lived to see his country under the power of foreigners. His teacher Socrates was put to death in 399 B.C. whereupon Plato, in company with Euclid and other 'disciples', fled to Megara, which lay about mid-way between Athens and Corinth. A year later Plato travelled extensively and visited Egypt, Italy and Sicily, where he was befriended by the ruler Dionysius. On his return Plato was captured by pirates and held to ransom. He can therefore be said to have been a man of good education and considerable experience, so that great things might be expected of his teaching at the

[1] In this, and all subsequent chapters, the single quote sign (') refers to minutes of arc, and the double quote sign (") to seconds of arc.

Academy[1] which he established in Athens in 387 at the age of forty. Plato spent the remainder of his days at the Academy, and died in 347 B.C. The Academy was, clearly, a delightful place; it was walled, and contained a grove of olive trees. Plato lived in the vicinity and used the Academy as a regular meeting place – it became in fact the first real place set aside for higher education. Teachers and pupils studied in a harmony of common interest but without the problem of formal qualifications – perhaps then the ideal surroundings and attitude of mind in which to work and something which in the modern world there is more than a tendency to lose. But whatever one may feel, at least we now have a background against which the story of the prowess of Greek astronomy may unfold.

Plato is remembered mainly for his writings on Socrates, on education, criticisms of sophistry, on politics and law and on philosophy. His cosmological views are not without interest, and certainly exerted considerable influence. First Plato took the view that the Earth was spherical, and then began to marry together geometry and nature into a widely-embracing system. The spherical Earth was placed in the centre of the universe, and no means of support was postulated. Plato was obviously of the opinion that so central and ideal a position was sufficient reason. On the other hand the planets were placed into circular orbits around the Earth. This whole scheme was tied in with his metaphysics. He was always seeking ultimate 'reality'. This reality was not directly to be perceived, for it was the essence which lay behind the material things which we see around us. Thus while men might speak of, say, an ox they would really only refer to the apparent oxen which they see at work; *ox* really refers to an idea of ox which is eternal, divinely created and thus unique. The oxen men see are then merely imperfect examples

---

[1] So called because the land on which it was established was originally the possession of the 'hero' Academos.

of the essential ox. From such an outlook as this it followed that the important duty of the philosopher was to examine essentials, and observation of the world around was, we might almost say, a sideline. Now to Plato the intelligence was the means man has to appreciate the essence of things; his senses merely provide him with knowledge of the changeable imperfect examples of divine and eternal archetypes. Moreover, the soul was immortal, and hence not of the changing world. Because of this approach Plato taught that the 'world' possessed a soul and intelligence, that it was a living entity. The fixed stars were divine and eternal creatures. The planets move in circles; after all, what more suitable – or should we say more 'perfect' – a path? In addition their distances were, Plato believed, related in a numerical way. To him numbers were, in a sense, true knowledge; and clearly, then, he had a *raison d'être* for this supposed connexion, which was made up of the two geometrical progressions 1, 2, 4, 8 and 1, 3, 9, 27. Combining the series and setting each digit by the planets in order from the Earth we obtain: Moon = 1, Sun = 2, Venus = 3, Mercury = 4, Mars = 8, Jupiter = 9, and Saturn = 27. By interpolating other numbers in a certain manner Plato forms an arithmetic musical scale which contains four Pythagorean octaves and a major sixth.[1] Unlike Pythagoras, Plato did not imagine that the planets emitted actual musical sounds; he was more concerned with the essential harmony which this system provided.

With Plato we may well claim that we have a not very scientific system, but at least he provided a self-consistent philosophical approach. And what is at least equally important, his conception of the changing apparent world and the unchanging essential reality had a deep influence on those whose ideas we shall now examine, and indeed on philosophers of other nations who followed much later still. The idea of celestial harmony and the unchanging nature of the

[1] For further discussion of such ideas see Appendix III.

celestial universe meant that uniform circular motions were the only satisfactory explanation for the behaviour of the Sun, Moon, and planets. However, the planets did not and do not behave exactly as they should do if simple uniform circular motions were the only factor governing their behaviour. In consequence subsequent Greek philosophers were concerned primarily with finding a system within the spherical universe whereby uniform circular motion could account for the temporary retrograde paths and stationary points which the planets exhibited. In doing so they showed incredible ingenuity.

The first new step in dealing with the problem was made by Eudoxus of Cnidos. Eudoxus was born *c.* 408 B.C., and went as a young man to attend Plato's academy. After this he travelled to Egypt and the area around the Sea of Marmara, and then returned to the area of Cnidos where he died *c.* 355 B.C. Eudoxus was a brilliant mathematician. He was responsible for the fifth book of 'Euclid', and invented the powerful method of exhaustion[1] which enabled a solution to be obtained to many problems which otherwise would have required the use of what, virtually, would have been a form of the calculus. Moreover, he propounded a general theory of proportion which was extremely significant for Greek mathematics of this time, and was later developed by Euclid in his great geometrical synthesis. In astronomy Eudoxus was also a great innovator, and made an attempt to account for planetary motions by his system of concentric or, more strictly, homocentric spheres. This was certainly an ingenious and elegant solution allowing of uniform circular motions as an explanation of complex planetary motions. The general idea was that every planet (including of course the Sun and Moon) was fixed to the equator of a sphere which rotated about its axis at uniform speed. The axis of each planetary sphere was carried by a larger sphere which

[1] A method of solution obtained by eliminating alternatives.

also rotated with a uniform velocity but about a different axis. Should the observed planetary motion not be satisfactorily accounted for in this way, then other spheres were postulated. In fact three spheres were used for the Sun and three for the Moon, and four for each of the planets, with one sphere to account for the diurnal rotation of the stars. For example, for the Moon the innermost sphere rotated once per month from west to east with its axis inclined 5° to the ecliptic, another rotated with an eighteen-year period in an east to west direction with its axis perpendicular to the ecliptic and an outermost sphere, with its axis coincident with the Earth's polar axis, rotated from east to west once in twenty-four hours. The planets each had an innermost sphere rotating east to west once every twenty-four hours with its axis coincident with that of the Earth, another rotating from west to east with its axis perpendicular to the ecliptic and spinning with a velocity equal to that of the planet's sidereal period, while two outer spheres accounted for the apparent loop or hippopede, rotating with the planet's synodic period, the outermost with its axis at an angle to the ecliptic and the other with its axis lying in the plane of the ecliptic. Thus Eudoxus found that a total of twenty-seven spheres was necessary. Each set of spheres was a separate 'entity', but it does not seem likely that he believed in their material existence; probably he looked on them as what they were, a mathematical solution to 'save the phenomena', as explanations accounting for planetary motions were called. The system was not satisfactory for Mars, and did not account either for eclipses or for the apparent changes in size of the Sun and Moon. Nevertheless it was a bold and important step forward. Eudoxus also proposed a calendar based on a four-year solar cycle with three years each of 365 days and one of 366 days, but this was not generally adopted until introduced in Rome three hundred years later by Julius Cæsar.

Aristotle, one of the Greek philosophers who is best remembered in the Western world, was born in 384 B.C. in the city of Stageira on the peninsula in which Mount Athos is situated, an area which at the time was still Ionian in outlook and independence. Aristotle was educated in Macedonia and Athens, and his father was physician to Amyntas, the Macedonian king. Aristotle studied under Plato, and while early in his life was a strong supporter of Platonic ideas, he later seceded from the Academy and in 335 B.C. founded the Lyceum in Athens. All but one of Aristotle's writings which have come down to us in their entirety originate in the latter part of his life, and may therefore be taken as expressing his maturer views. In his scientific endeavours it must be remembered that Aristotle's greatest contributions lay in the biological sciences. These were, however, not properly appreciated until the nineteenth century A.D. and it is his cosmological system which really had a profound influence on later developments. Aristotle believed that the Earth was in the centre of the universe, and he was certain that it was completely stationary. He produced a number of arguments to prove that the earth was spherical, quoting the observed facts that different constellations were observed by travellers who voyaged north and south, that falling bodies always fell perpendicularly to the Earth's surface wheresoever dropped (the sphere being the one geometrical figure which would allow of this) and that during a lunar eclipse the Earth's shadow is seen to be a section of a sphere. The order which he adopted for the planets was the Moon, Mercury and Venus, the Sun, Mars, Jupiter and Saturn; for explaining their motions Aristotle adopted the Eudoxian concept of homocentric spheres, but he looked on them as truly physical, and made certain modifications which raised the total number of spheres to fifty-five. The sphere of the fixed stars carried out only the diurnal east to west motion, but metaphysically this was satisfactory because many stars had one motion while a few stars (the planets) had many motions. Aristotle discussed the size of the earth, although he himself made no measurements, merely using the method of a star's altitude as observed from different latitudes when the distance between the places of observation was known. He obtained a value of 12,461 miles[1] for the Earth's diameter, and considered also that the stars themselves were larger than this.

Aristotle taught that the heavens, that is to say the regions above the sphere of the Moon, were changeless. It was here that uniform circular motion and perpetual order reigned. Change was confined to the sub-lunar regions, where motion in a straight line could take place. In this region the four elements earth, air, fire and water and the four qualities wet, dry, hot and cold were to be found. The elements were not, of course, to be identified with the everyday substances of earth, air, fire and water; the natural materials were pale imitations of the essential elements, and thus the ethical purity of the heavens could even penetrate to the changing world where mankind lived. By the middle of the fourth century B.C. the transitory phenomena observed in the heavens, shooting stars, comets, haloes, clouds, rainbows, auroræ and thunder and lightning, had so impinged on the province of the natural philosopher that some explanation for them was required. These Aristotle dealt with in his *Meteorologica*, and classified all of them as phenomena occurring in the upper air, supposing that shooting stars (which later came to be called 'meteors') and comets were the ignited hot and dry products of evaporation. Comets, and indeed meteors, had for long been believed to be portents

---

[1] This is assuming that the Greek stadium was equal to 157·5 metres. Our knowledge of its value comes from Pliny the Younger, who recorded that 40 stadia were taken, by Eratosthenes at least, as equal to a σχοινος. The σχοινος was adopted from the Egyptians and was equal to 12,000 royal cubits, that is 6,300 metres (1 cubit = 0·525 m.). Hence 40 stadia = 6,300 m. or 1 stadium = 157·5 m.

of disaster and harbingers of pestilence and disease, and it is obvious that Aristotle's physical explanation would give a *raison d'être* at least for epidemics which occurred under hot and dry conditions. The Milky Way was taken to be caused by the motion of the sphere of the fixed stars. This explained why it always appeared in the same position relative to them; its nature was believed to be an accumulation of ignited vapour, and because of the quantity of such vapour it required the amount left over and available to form comets was small – hence the comparative rarity of the latter. Whatever we may now know, we cannot but admit that this explanation by Aristotle was both ingenious and self-consistent. As far as the size of the universe was concerned, Aristotle rejected the idea that it was infinite in extent. Spheres of infinite size could not exist; therefore he believed the universe to be finite, and that outside the sphere of the fixed stars was a sphere, the so-called 'primum mobile', which was moved by the Deity himself and the source of all motions in the universe.

A different planetary arrangement and the idea of a diurnal rotation of the Earth entered Greek astronomy through the efforts of Heracleides of Pontus, who was a wealthy man, and was born in Heracleia Pontica on the southern shores of the Black Sea in about 388 B.C. Heracleides was a great admirer of Empedocles, and conceived of the universe as made up of jointless particles. He has sometimes been referred to as the Greek Tycho in view of his planetary system which was heliocentric for the inferior planets Mercury and Venus, and geocentric for the remainder. Such a comparison is both incorrect and silly. Tycho's planetary system was indeed a cross between the already proposed heliocentric views of Copernicus and the geocentric system of antiquity, but the proposals of Heracleides were a first step forward from the geocentric system and were, in fact, an entirely new approach. It is unfortunate that the ingenuity of Heracleides did not find favour. His concept of the diurnal rotation of the Earth was too novel a departure from the general outlook, from what we may rightly term the 'scientific climate' of the day. Moreover, although this is not often realized today, it was not supported by observational evidence. However, Heracleides was not alone in being a philosopher who tried to put forward ideas of a novel kind about the universe. At about the same time as Heracleides flourished, Apollonius of Perga and Aristarchus of Samos, whose work was carried out in the second half of the third century B.C., also made attempts to bring forward really new ideas.

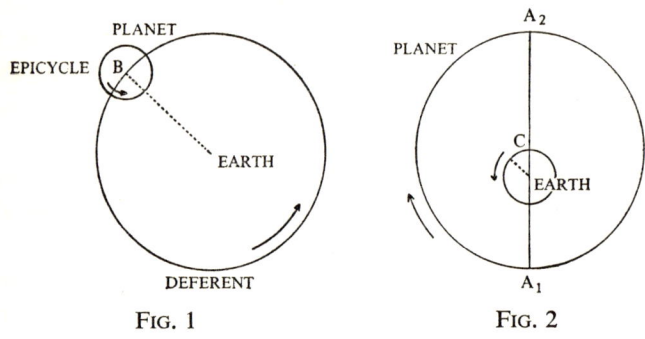

Fig. 1 Fig. 2

Apollonius is, of course, well known for his theoretical work on conic sections. Astronomically he proposed, or at least certainly used, alternative methods to the homocentric spheres to account for planetary motion. These were the methods of epicycles (fig. 1) – still with us in the form of the epicyclic gear – and the movable excentric (fig. 2). Both are ingenious geometrical ways of combining uniform circular motion to give a resultant which can 'save the phenomena' and account for the apparent peculiarities of planetary behaviour.[1]

The epicyclic system in due course supplanted the movable excentric, probably because it could be used to account for

[1] See Appendix II.

GREEK IDEAS – SECOND PHASE

the motion of all the planets while the movable excentric applied to the superior planets only. Both these systems were mathematical devices. The movable excentric was an elegant solution but with it the epicycle and deferent had still to be used to account for the motions of Mercury and Venus. Ptolemy used the epicyclic system exclusively and this was followed until the advent of Kepler's elliptical orbits. Apollonius was well aware that the movable excentric could be transformed into the epicyclic. With the movable excentric it was generally accepted that the point C represented the Sun, and in consequence it led to a kind of heliocentric system; but on the other hand, there was no need to use it. The gradual supplanting of the movable excentric by the deferent and epicycle therefore removed any emphasis which might have led to the adoption of a full-blown heliocentric system.

Aristarchus of Samos seems to have been the real protagonist of heliocentric views, and a brief sketch must now be given of his cosmological system. He believed the star sphere to be motionless and he placed the Sun at its centre. The planets, and the Earth also, were taken to travel in movable excentrics round the Sun as centre. The system was truly a heliocentric one. He appreciated that if this scheme were to be the real one then some explanation of the apparent changelessness of the stars was required. He therefore sagely realized that the radius of the sphere of the fixed stars must be immensely greater than the radius of the Earth's orbit, and taught that this was so.

Aristarchus also made an ingenious attempt to determine the distances of the Sun and the Moon. He observed the Moon when in quadrature (fig. 3) and measured the elongation of the Sun (the angle MES), obtaining the value of 87°. From the angles in the triangle, Aristarchus found the ratio of the distances of Earth to Moon (EM) and Earth to Sun (ES). The value he obtained lay between 1:18 and

1:20.[1] His measurement of the Sun's elongation was, however, too small and as such a kind of observation as he attempted is difficult, considering the instruments available to him, his result was better than one might have expected. Indeed Aristarchus is much to be commended for the work he did and the result he obtained, but he himself appreciated its inadequacy and he suggested another method which was later used by Hipparchus and which we shall discuss presently. Aristarchus obtained a value for the ratio for the sizes of the Sun and Moon of 20:18.

Measurement seems to have been in vogue amongst Greek

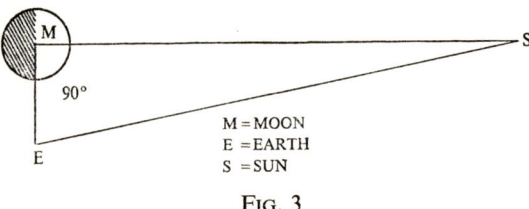

FIG. 3

astronomers of this period, due a little perhaps to the influence of the Stoic philosophy which had grown up in the fourth century B.C. under Zeno. It was a practical philosophy, and set great store by mental training. The Stoics believed in an all-pervading primary substance which co-exists with matter, and by variation in its tension causes different physical properties. Although not a philosophy promoting physical science it was a useful antidote to Platonic ideas. Eratosthenes, librarian of the great museum at Alexandria, determined to make as accurate a measure of the size of the Earth as was possible. This he did by measuring the length of the solar shadow at Alexandria and the distance between Alexandria and Syene. Syene lay on the tropic of Cancer, so that at summer solstice the Sun lay directly overhead and

[1] The Greeks had no sine tables and, in consequence, Aristarchus could not find exactly the ratio EM : ES.

a vertical gnomon cast no shadow at all; Syene was, of course, on the same meridian as Alexandria. In effect Eratosthenes measured the difference in latitude between Alexandria and Syene. The distance was measured in stadia. From the evidence of Pliny the Younger it seems that Eratosthenes adopted a value of 516 feet $8\frac{3}{4}$ inches for the stadium. The distance between Alexandria and Syene amounted to 5,300 stadia, and with the length of the solar shadow at Alexandria, the value for the Earth's circumference worked out as 24,662 miles, giving a diameter of 7,850 miles. This differed but 50 miles from the present-day value for the polar diameter. Eratosthenes also made careful measures of the obliquity of the ecliptic again using the gnomon.[1]

This tradition of measurement was carried on by Hipparchus of Nicæa, who flourished around 150 B.C. Although born at Nicæa he spent most of his life in Rhodes, a flourishing city-state noted for its maritime prowess and the many works of art, among which was the Colossus, a giant statue, which was known as one of the seven wonders of the ancient world. Virtually all the writings of Hipparchus are lost, but from the reports of others, and not least the work of Ptolemy, much of what he did can be ascertained; it is clear that he can properly he termed the greatest observational astronomer of antiquity. He was the first philosopher to compile a catalogue of stars. He observed down to the sixth magnitude, and his catalogue contained 850 stars, co-ordinates of which were measured from the ecliptic as a basic reference; in other words their positions were given in terms of celestial longitudes and latitudes. He compared his value

---

[1] The method is as follows:

a_w = altitude at winter solstice = $(90° - \phi) - \omega$ where ϕ = latitude and ω = obliquity

a_s = altitude at summer solstice = $\omega + (90° - \phi)$

∴ $\frac{1}{2}(a_s - a_w) = \omega$.

for the position of α Virginis (Spica) with the observed position given some century and a half earlier by Timocharis and Aristillus in Alexandria, and he concluded that the difference of position, which amounted to more than 2°, was too great to be put down to observational errors. He checked some other star positions and concluded that the relative positions of the ecliptic and celestial equators had changed, and he believed, correctly, that this was a secular phenomenon. He had, in fact, discovered precession. His careful observations also led him to discover that the sidereal year was 20 minutes longer than the tropical year, a correction which was amazingly accurate.[1] He also set about measuring the relative distance of the Sun, both from eclipse data as suggested by Aristarchus and from careful measurement of the length of the seasons. From these measurements he found that the solar parallax was 2′ 54″. This was still too large a value but a definite improvement over previous determinations; indeed although almost 20 times as great as the modern value it was a bold attempt and, as we shall see when considering astronomy of the seventeenth century, the exact measurement of this quantity still taxed the ingenuity of astronomers, being only successfully evaluated in the eighteenth century by Laplace who used gravitational methods.

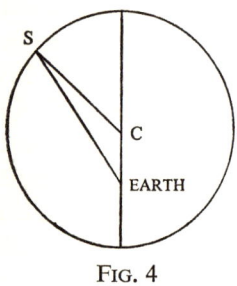

FIG. 4

These achievements would be more than enough to ensure Hipparchus a permanent place in a history of astronomy. Moreover, he showed an astoundingly modern scientific attitude in his approach to the problem of the motion of the Sun. To account for observations, Hipparchus favoured the fixed excentric (fig. 4) in which the Sun S moves with uniform motion around the centre C. From the Earth E the Sun

[1] Present value about 25 minutes 25 seconds longer.

GREEK IDEAS – SECOND PHASE

describes a path of non-uniform angular velocity which, of course, fits in well with its observed seasonal variation. For discussing the Moon's motion he used the device of the movable excentric. Although he recognized the synodic month, the sidereal month (the Moon's return to the same position among the fixed stars), the anomalistic month (the Moon's return from perigee to perigee – that is from A_1 to A_1 again in fig. 2) and the draconitic or nodical month (the Moon's crossing of the celestial equator to the point of crossing again), the fixed excentric did not really satisfy his observations. Nor could he 'save the phenomena' in a way satisfactory to himself by using either the movable excentric or the deferent and epicycle. He therefore confined himself to observations of the planets' positions and said that he left the solution of the problem of planetary motion to his successors, being of the opinion that no theory available to him or which he could devise was satisfactory enough. What a balanced, humble and scientific outlook Hipparchus must have had. If only others who followed had indeed appreciated this attitude and taken heed! Yet the history of science is full of 'ifs' and 'buts', and it is profitless to spend time romancing on them – it is only profitable to learn to apply them to ourselves in such investigations as may now concern us.

The last and probably the most influential of the Greek natural philosophers who was concerned with astronomy, was Claudius Ptolemæus (Ptolemy). He flourished in the second century A.D., but little is known of his life. It is believed that he was born in the city Ptolemais Hermii, but his main work was carried out in Alexandria, where he certainly made astronomical observations between 128 and 145 A.D. Later traditions say that Ptolemy died at the age of seventy-eight. Although remembered primarily for his astronomical endeavours, Ptolemy also worked on geographical problems, with special reference to the relative positions of places and map projections, and produced an atlas of the ancient world. In mathematics he showed himself to be a geometrician of the first rank. He concerned himself with a new proof on the Euclidean postulate on parallel lines and a theorem concerning a quadrilateral inscribed in a circle, and from this he demonstrated concisely and elegantly how a table of chords might be drawn up. He wrote on music and on optics, and made the first attempt to tackle the knotty problem of the refraction of heavenly bodies. His main astronomical work is enshrined in his magnum opus *The Almagest*,[1] which gives his own views and ideas as well as recording those of Hipparchus.

Ptolemy taught a thorough-going geocentric system, using the system of deferents and epicycles. Moreover, he gave many arguments in favour of keeping the Earth stationary and in the centre of the universe. Ptolemy therefore seems to have considered the possibilities of a heliocentric system, but it was for logical reasons that he emphatically promoted the geocentric hypothesis. In his favour it must be realized that he had the most important of all factors to support him – observation. The system of deferents and epicycles did explain the observed phenomena within the limits of accuracy of observation, at least to a degree which appeared satisfactory and gave promise of even closer correlation in time to come. Observational evidence for motion of the Earth was not obtained for over sixteen hundred years, although as we shall see, the geocentric concept was overthrown in the sixteenth century for other reasons. It must not be thought, then, as it often seems to be, that Ptolemy was blind to views other than his own. Nor must one fall into the trap of thinking that Ptolemy was not a practical observer. Hipparchus was no doubt a more able observational astronomer, but Ptolemy

[1] *The Almagest* is not the original title of the work. It was originally called *The Mathematical Collection* which became known as *The Great Astronomer*. In the ninth century the Arabian astronomers referred to the work by the word 'greatest' or in Greek $\mu\varepsilon\gamma\iota\sigma\tau\eta$ (megistee) which, with the definite article 'al' prefixed, led to the title *Almagest*.

GREEK IDEAS – SECOND PHASE

himself extended Hipparchus' star catalogue and included a total of 1,022 stars. His observing instruments were probably similar to those of Hipparchus. For determining the meridian altitude of the Sun he used an arm with open sights pivoted about one end, the arm moving against a square board on which a quadrant divided into 90° was inscribed, the instrument having a plumb line adjustment (fig. 5a). For stellar observations he used an armillary sphere – here graduated circles were set parallel to those 'on' the celestial sphere and the star positions, in terms of celestial longitude and latitude, were read off using pointers with open sights. He also used a device (fig. 5b) which again was probably used by Hipparchus although it came to be called 'Ptolemy's Rules', by means of which one could ascertain the zenith distance of a star.

Ptolemy made substantial advances in the theory of the motion of the Moon. He found that a deferent with centre coincident with the centre of the Earth was not satisfactory. He therefore considered the errors which existed between theory and observation and, realizing that these sometimes reached a maximum at quadrature and always vanished at syzygy,[1] he concluded that there were two errors of motion which must be accounted for. The first gave an effect as if the radius of the epicycle were variable, the second[2] as if the centre of the epicycle were not moving on a deferent centred on the Earth. Ptolemy's solution was to use a deferent with its centre a little distance from the centre of the Earth E (fig. 6) and an epicycle the uniform angular motion of which was uniform about another point N. The point N was situated on the opposite of the Earth to the centre of the deferent C, and the distance CE was taken as equal to the distance EN. In this arrangement the apogee was not taken to be on a

---

[1] The Moon is said to be in syzygy when Sun, Moon and Earth are in the same straight line.
[2] Now known as *evection*.

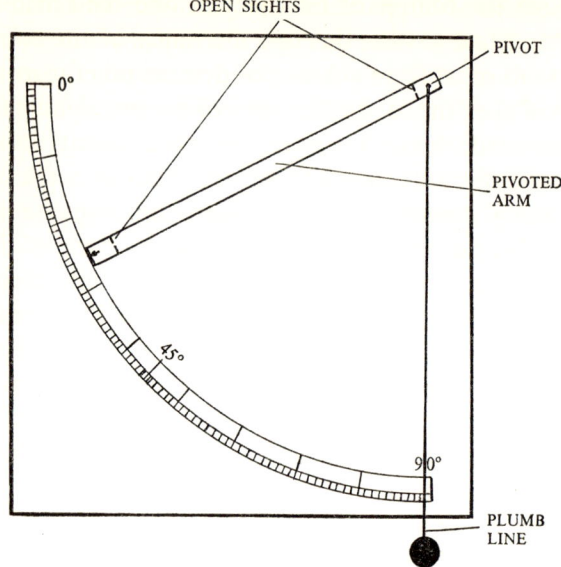

Fig. 5a

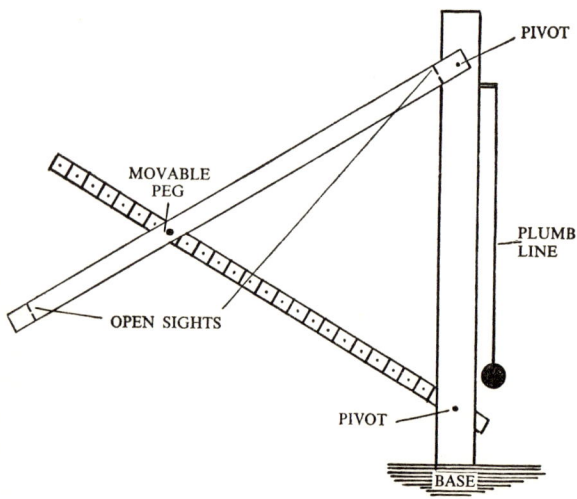

Fig. 5b

GREEK IDEAS – SECOND PHASE

line through the centres of the epicycle and the Earth but, instead, on a line passing through the centre of the epicycle and the point of uniform angular motion; in other words the apogee was at A (fig. 6) on the line NB produced instead of at A'. This solution was, however, only partially satisfactory. It was certainly an improvement on previous work, and Ptolemy found himself unable to better it although he made attempts to do so.

For planetary motions Ptolemy adopted a similar system, again using an eccentrically situated deferent. The situation of the point of uniform angular motion, N, and known as the *equant*, was different to that adopted for the Moon. The

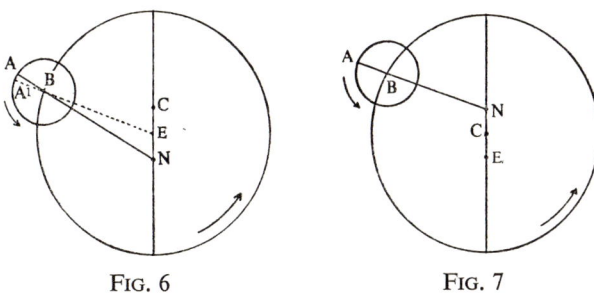

Fig. 6   Fig. 7

equant lay on the opposite side of C to the Earth E (fig. 7). Moreover, Ptolemy assumed that the deferents for the various planets were inclined to the plane of the ecliptic, and the planes of the epicycles by an equal but opposite amount, and to account for the then known inequalities, the planes of the deferents and epicycles were believed to oscillate by the total amounts of their inclinations. The planet Mercury raised special problems. To account for its observed behaviour the equant was supposed to be situated between the centre of the Earth and the centre of the deferent and, in addition, the centre of the deferent was taken as describing a small circle about another point which lay close to the equant.

In brief, then, Ptolemy tried to tackle the thorny problems

involved in saving the phenomena by using every ingenuity he could devise while still keeping to a geocentric hypothesis and uniform circular motions. His system was nowhere so simple as is generally supposed. However, his attempt was brilliant indeed and satisfied many generations of astronomers; indeed, the tables he prepared of planetary motions held their own until the geocentric theory was overthrown in the sixteenth century. Ptolemy appreciated that the planets were much closer to the Earth than were the fixed stars, but seems to have believed that the epicycles were solid and rotated in between actual crystalline spheres. He also wrote on astrology, a subject on which Greek astronomers had, in general, but little to say.

Comets, as has been said, were classified as meteorological phenomena. This was a necessary concomitant of the generally held view that the heavens and everything in them – everything above the sphere of the Moon, that is – suffered no change. Comets were transitory phenomena, and at best appeared for a few months; therefore they must, according to the general cosmological views, lie in the sphere of change and be phenomena of the upper air. Admittedly there had been earlier theories of the physical nature of comets. Of these, two put forward the idea that comets were merely optical illusions, one suggesting that they were due to reflected sunlight, the other that they were caused by close planetary conjunctions. A third opinion considered comets to be true phenomena but to have only a short period of life – the Pythagoreans claiming that comets were errant stars. The meteorological hypothesis was put forward first by Heracleides in the fourth century B.C. and was certainly the generally held view, in spite of a minority opinion of Anaxogoras and Democritus, who considered comets to be eternal and suggested that they made temporary appearances according to laws which were not understood. Greek observations were primarily concerned with the physical appearance of comets themselves, a classification being based according to the shape, length, colour and brightness of the tail.

The influence of Greek philosophers lasted for very many centuries after their civilization had passed away as a political power. If we consider the state of astronomical knowledge when the Greek philosophers entered on the scene, the great steps made in mathematical analysis of planetary motions, the logical arguments used to support the various hypotheses, and the cosmological hypotheses themselves, we can surely only stand back and admire. Here, in the eastern Mediterranean, we can see the beginnings of that mathematical-observational-hypothetical approach to problems of the cosmos which characterizes modern astronomy. The techniques may sometimes appear crude; the contribution of previous civilizations cannot be neglected; yet the developments of astronomy in the able hands of Greek philosophers are a great tribute to the genius of the human mind. That later generations, as we shall see in the next chapter, allowed these views to act as a brake on independent thought and development is indeed unfortunate, but we do ill to lay this at the door of a civilization which forged ahead on the adventure of astronomical discovery.

Chapter 5

ISLAM AND THE GROWTH OF ASTRONOMY IN WESTERN CHRISTENDOM

After the work of Ptolemy, the development of astronomy came to a standstill. Other philosophers who flourished in Alexandria seemed satisfied in preparing commentaries on the views of Hipparchus and Ptolemy; the urge to adventure further in the realms of original thought appeared to have died. Developments did occur in the mathematical field, but any new tools which were thus developed were never applied to the problems of cosmology. Seneca and Pliny the Younger wrote on astronomy but their work was not original, they only recorded the traditions and views of earlier generations of philosophers.

Astrology became rife, and besides the work of Seneca and Pliny, which occurred in the first century A.D., there seem to be no other references to Greek views, except in so far as commentaries on Hipparchus and Ptolemy can be taken to be references to a development of thought which had passed. An age of scientific stultification set in. Worse was to follow. The Alexandrian school of philosophers, of which Ptolemy was the most shining example, had, by the fifth century, received their first real death blow by the destruction of a branch of the great library at Alexandria. This was carried out by a mob which brutally murdered Hypatia, a mathematician and daughter of Theon, and then set about the library, all at the instigation of the patriarch Cyril. This was in line with the early Christian attitude which, literally, fought against what was believed to be heresy, and showed little interest in knowledge for its own sake. Such an outlook was typified, for example, by St Ambrose who wrote: '... To discuss the nature and position of the Earth does not help us in our hope of the life to come.' Christians, after waiting for the second coming of Christ and finding that their sojourn on the Earth was to be more extended than they had supposed, turned their concern to matters of behaviour and discipline designed to fit them for the eternal life which was their hope. To those who subscribed to such a view this was clearly more important than apparently idle questions of natural philosophy. As far back as the first century A.D., St Paul had also expressed a similar view in his contempt for Greek theological inquiry when he criticized the Athenians for their dedicatory inscription 'to the unknown God'. This outlook grew, gathered strength and, finally, prevailed. Later, however, it was Christian scholars who began, in the eleventh and twelfth centuries, to redress the balance for Western civilization.

The final death blow to Alexandrian culture came with the conquests by Islam in the seventh century. In 640 the Alexandrian library was finally destroyed at the command of the Caliph Omar. Omar was a fanatic. He took the incontrovertible attitude that either the works contained in the library were in agreement with the teachings enshrined in the Koran – in which case they were superfluous – or they opposed the Koran and were, therefore, heretical. In either case destruction was the one course open to a true follower of the Prophet. With the final destruction of the library astronomical endeavour died, or at least went into cold storage. Bigotry and lethargy prevailed. From the second century to the ninth, astronomy, in all but its astrological guise, made no progress whatever.

Islamic conquest continued and the followers of the Prophet pressed westwards. However, in 732, after the battle of Tours, things began to settle down and the sons of Islam had time to consolidate their successes. They also had time to turn to the study of cultural matters. Because the Koran, and thus the whole Mohammedan faith, used a lunar calendar, the Caliphs were stimulated to look with favour on those who would attend to the problem of a luni-solar calendar and thus on the study of astronomy. In spite of the two attacks on the library at Alexandria, some works had been hidden and escaped the tragic destruction which befell the others. In the eighth century these treasures made their way into the open, at first in Baghdad. Here the Caliph Haroun-al-Rashid, immortalized in the *Arabian Nights* and in Flecker's *Hassan*, flourished, and the Caliph Al-mamun established a 'house of wisdom'. Ptolemy's *Almagest* was translated into Arabic in 820, and this immediately coloured the work that followed on determining the size of the Earth from observations of meridian arcs, and on the obliquity of the ecliptic.

In the ninth century there flourished two notable astronomers, Tabit-ben-Korra and Al-Battani (whose name was later Latinized to Albategnius). Both read the works of the Greeks which had by that time become available, and both carried out careful observations. Tabit-ben-Korra was dissatisfied at the details of planetary motion as received from Greek sources. He proposed an oscillation of the ecliptic which, of course, resulted in a fluctuation in the point of its intersection with the celestial equator, that is the vernal equinox. This oscillation was known as *trepidation* and appeared to offer an explanation by means of which the phenomena of planetary motion could the better be accounted for. He accepted the reality of the celestial spheres and the deferent and epicycle. Al-Battani did not accept trepidation but, after determining the direction of the apse line of the Sun's orbit[1] and finding a difference of 16° 47′

[1] The line NBA in fig. 7 (p. 73) where A = the Sun.

ISLAM AND CHRISTENDOM

between his determination and that of Ptolemy, appreciated that a secular rotation of this apse line[1] would account for the errors observed by Tabit-ben-Korra. It is clear that Al-Battani was a careful and meticulous observer, for not only did he make his proposals about the rotation of the apse line, but also he re-determined the rate of precession and also, with considerable accuracy, the obliquity of the ecliptic.

In the tenth century the science of Islam was still in the ascendant but information began to filter through to the Christian civilization of the west. Some bold and brave spirits learned Arabic and visited Seville, Cordova and Toledo. Here they began to become acquainted with the Greek philosophers but the development of science was slow and it is to Islam that we must turn to watch the progress of astronomy. The last of the Baghdad astronomers was Abul Wefa who, like his predecessors, also made careful observations and who thereby discovered a third correction to the Moon's motion. This is known as the *variation*; it takes account of the apparently advanced position of the Moon between new moon and the first quarter, and between the last quarter and full moon. Unfortunately due to too great a reverence for Greek work, and especially that of Ptolemy, this discovery was not properly appreciated and Abul Wefa's efforts seem to have had no lasting effect.

The eleventh and twelfth centuries were a period of little significance astronomically, but in the thirteenth century a brief revival took place. Hulagu Khan, a Mongol, captured Baghdad and founded an observatory at Merâgha which his vizier, Nassir-al-Din, supervised. Here the amount of precession was determined with great accuracy. In 1420 an observatory was also founded at Samarkand by the ill-fated Ulugh Beg, grandson of Tamerlane. Here instruments of

[1] We now accept a secular motion of the apse line of the *Earth's* orbit.

enormous dimensions were used like those of the observatory at Jaipur in India. Ulugh Beg also obtained improved values for the obliquity of the ecliptic and for precession but his great claim to fame lies in the star catalogue he prepared, the first of its kind since that of Ptolemy, thirteen hundred years before. However, work at Samarkand ceased when Ulugh Beg was murdered for political reasons.

The Islamic approach was clearly one of precise measurement. Many astronomical constants were carefully redetermined and so provided information of vital use for those who followed on in Western Christendom. Indeed, by the end of the tenth century the Muslim astronomer Ibn-Yunus, who worked in Egypt, had computed a set of planetary tables named the Hakemite tables after his patron the Caliph Al-Hakim, but these were superseded in the eleventh century by the Toledan tables which were prepared in Toledo by Jewish astronomers working under Moslem masters. Cosmologically the Muslims contributed nothing original – such speculations do not appear to have interested or stimulated them – instead they were content to accept the hypotheses proposed by the Greeks and in so doing acted as torchbearers, handing on this ancient legacy to Western Christendom where, in the years to come, it was to be melted down and cast in new patterns. In addition to measures of precision Islamic astronomers handed on to the west many Arabic astronomical terms such as the star names Aldebaran, Altair and Betelgeuse and the technical terms almanac, almucantar, nadir and zenith. It is also to Islam that we shall ever be in debt for the introduction of trigonometry and the so-called Arabic numerals. These numerals had a profound effect which it is difficult to over-emphasize. With their radix of ten, their positional factor, and a sign for zero they had an immense influence, and represented a great advance on the cumbersome Greek and Roman systems. They seem first to have been put to work in the ninth century by Alkarizmi from whom the word 'algebra' is also derived.[1] We should also find it difficult to stress too much the importance of trigonometry. This mathematical 'technique', especially in the form of spherical trigonometry, the foundations of which were laid by Al-Battani, is extremely useful in problems of positional astronomy and navigation. Even, then, if we cannot look to Islam for any contributions which changed man's general views of the universe, we do well to remember our debt to them for the introduction of measures and techniques which were the raw material for the further developments we shall now trace.

As we have already said the early Christian attitude was primarily a fight against heresies – those doctrines either believed to be heretical or likely to militate against the faith. Of the Church Fathers, each had his own attitude to the teachings of Greek science, the earlier tending to be more liberally minded than the later ones who, after persecution, hardened in their attitude to all that was part of the pagan world. Origen (185–254) and others who came from the cultured city of Alexandria were more favourably disposed to those teachings which were concerned with matters of nature. However, the entire outlook and the acceptance or rejection of astronomical doctrines were conditioned by the relationship they appeared to have to Christian teaching. Thus deterministic astrology, being concerned with the future of emperors, states and persons, was considered heretical because it denied free-will, although natural astrology, which dealt only with physical phenomena such as tides, was permitted; the doctrine of cycles of recurrence of events in the universe (*palingenesis*), and Aristotle's idea of the eternal existence of the universe, were condemned as heresy; on the other hand there was in general a tendency to accept the

[1] Alkarizmi used the term *ilma al-jabr w'al muquabalah* meaning the science of 'reduction and cancelling out', the literal translation of *al-jabr* being 'transferring terms'.

facts of observation and the Greek ideas of planetary motion. By the fourth century there was growing an independence of thought which, however, augured ill for astronomy. Practical observation was not carried out systematically, the idea of the spherical Earth was ridiculed, and concepts of the universe were put forward which were based on allegories of scripture. Some improvements began in the seventh century, there was a return to the hypothesis of a spherical Earth, but matters only really began to get under way in the twelfth century. This was the period when Arabic sources were tapped and original Greek writings, especially those of Aristotle, became translated into Latin by such scholars as Gerbert. Earlier the ethics of Aristotle had been known, but now his teaching on natural science was available for study and comment.

The thirteenth century saw the ripening of the fruits of these new sources of information. Differences between the views of Aristotle and Ptolemy were recognized to exist, and decisions had to be made or excuses found to get over this disagreement between such 'authorities'. St Thomas Aquinas approached the problem by attempting a synthesis of what he understood as Aristotle's thought, and the doctrines of the Christian faith. His attempt was successful, so much so that the synthesis became accepted as the true picture, and Aristotelian cosmology and physics became synonymous with orthodoxy. This had grave repercussions when, in the sixteenth and seventeenth centuries, the west came to stand on its own and new cosmological ideas began to emerge. During the thirteenth century John of Halifax (*alias* Sacrobosco) wrote a simple book on the sphere and on astronomy. This had a great vogue and copies even found their way into use as late as the seventeenth century. Matters moved slowly in those days and new advances did not always make themselves felt as quickly or as widely as is sometimes imagined.

As Western Christendom took up the study of astronomy, the problems of planetary motion were the first to be tackled.

In the fifteenth century original Greek texts had been recovered. The Greek language was studied so that, instead of relying on Latin translations of Arabic works, which were themselves derived from the Greek, the original sources could be studied. This attitude of mind, which desired to discover for itself and examine past work without preconceived ideas, was symptomatic of the new culture and the genesis of the new philosophical approach which was to have so startling an effect and place Western science in a position unique in the world's history. In Austria and Germany there arose at this period a school of astronomy of which the main figures were Georg Purbach (1423-1461), and Johannes Müller (1436-1476) who is better known by his latinized name Regiomontanus. Purbach carried on from where Sacrobosco had left off and, after careful studies of Latin translations of the *Almagest*, himself compiled a manual of astronomy. Regiomontanus and Purbach worked together on the *Almagest* in Rome and, after the early death of the latter, Regiomontanus stayed on, mastered Greek, and completed the Purbach manual. Regiomontanus finally settled down in Nuremberg where Bernard Walther became both his pupil and benefactor. Here they founded an observatory and a printing shop from which Purbach's book was published. Regiomontanus made many careful observations and invented a method of 'lunar distances' by means of which the coordinates of a ship at sea could, at least in theory, be determined from observations of the Moon. Almanacs and ephemerides were computed and published from Nuremberg, and the work was carried on by Walther after the death of Regiomontanus in Rome, whence he had gone to assist in the reform of the calendar. In Italy observations, not least of the six comets which appeared between 1433 and 1472, were made by Paolo Toscanelli (1397-1482) who also provided corrections to the Alphonsine tables, and by Nicholas of Cusa (1401-1464). Both Toscanelli and Nicholas were students of the great university of Padua which was, at this time, one of the leading centres of learning. It was here that Galileo was later to work. Nicholas of Cusa revived the teachings of the Pythagorean school and it is claimed that he also considered the possibility of a heliocentric theory. Leonardo da Vinci (1452–1519) gave some consideration to astronomical problems; he considered the stars to be far off and the Sun a large body which was exceedingly hot. He observed the face of the Moon, considering the dark areas to be dry land and the bright parts seas. Leonardo gave a correct explanation of earthshine (he termed it 'moon lustre'), although it would not appear that his idea was widely known because, for almost a century later, there was still much discussion among astronomers as to the real reason for the phenomenon. Perhaps his most advanced views concerned the Earth, which he considered to be in rotation, adducing evidence on falling bodies and their deflexion from the vertical as proof of his contention. Again, however, Leonardo's views do not seem to have exerted any wide influence.

The fifteenth century, then, shows clearly the growing independence of mind with which astronomers were tackling the problems which lay before them. The sixteenth century brought a culmination which appeared in the form of proposals of Nicholas Copernicus (1473–1543) for a heliocentric hypothesis. Copernicus was born in Torun in Poland and, after his father's death in 1483, was brought up by his maternal uncle who became bishop of Heilsberg. Copernicus studied first at the university of Cracow and then went to Italy. Here he took his doctorate in Canon law in Ferrara and studied medicine in Padua. It was in Italy that he came in touch with the neo-Pythagorean outlook on cosmology and was imbued with that attitude to planetary motions which sought the most elegant solution and eschewed the physical approach of Aristotle. Copernicus learned Greek and was able, therefore, to consult original sources. In reaching his conclusions Copernicus was keen to have observational evidence, and he constructed instruments after Ptolemy's designs and made his own observations. It seems likely that these were inferior in accuracy even to the later Greek observations of, for example, Hipparchus, and it is certain that his accuracy did not exceed 10'. He did not bring any critical approach to earlier observations and, because he insisted on taking all into account equally, his own theory had to be more complex than it would otherwise have been. Copernicus went over his theory again and again but he seemed loath to publish it, being content with a circulation of his views among his friends. However, Rhæticus, a protestant scholar from Wittenburg, came to study with Copernicus and, after working with him for 3 years, himself published in 1540 a summary, the *Narratio Prima*. Later Rhæticus prevailed on Copernicus to let him have the whole manuscript and take it to Nuremberg for publication. Rhæticus was however no longer in Nuremberg when publication took place and the work was finally seen through the press by Osiander, a Lutheran priest. Osiander wrote an additional preface in which he stressed the importance of the heliocentric theory as an improved calculating device for planetary motion, but implied that the motion of the Earth was not to be taken as a real phenomenon. This does not seem to have been Copernicus' outlook, indeed he had been in correspondence with Osiander on this whole aspect of the theory and had disagreed with the latter's views. However, the book was published in May 1543 with the title *De Revolutionibus Orbium Cœlestium* Libri VI,[1] was dedicated to the Pope and a copy is supposed to have reached Copernicus two hours before his death.

[1] The original manuscript has no title. As Dr Armitage has pointed out (Angus Armitage, *Sun, stand thou still*, London, 1947) we do not know what title Copernicus intended, but it is likely that the title *De Revolutionibus* would have sufficed, as Copernicus was no believer in the reality of the crystal spheres of antiquity.

The *De Revolutionibus* exerted a profound influence. As its full title explains it was divided into six books, in the first of which Copernicus used arguments similar to those of Aristotle, but to prove an opposite conclusion, namely that the Earth *does* move. Using this heliocentric hypothesis an explanation is given of the seasons and there are also included sections on trigonometry, together with a table of sines. The second book is concerned with spherical trigonometry and a catalogue of stars. The latter was of no great significance, being virtually that in the *Almagest* but corrected for precession. Book three gave a detailed theory of the Earth's motion, book four provided details of the Moon's motion, and in books five and six planetary motions were discussed. Copernicus still used the deferent and epicycle in order to account for minor inequalities in lunar and planetary motions but, because he used a stationary Sun, the deferents and epicycles of Ptolemy necessary to account for a stationary Earth were not required and the whole system of Copernicus was considerably less complex than any previous hypothesis. It was for this reason that the new theory became accepted – it eased considerably the labour of computation of ephemerides – for it must be remembered that there was, in the sixteenth century, no direct observational evidence for the motion of the Earth.

Much has been written and said about religious objections to the Copernican views. Objections there were but as many current opinions appear to be based more on what their originators wish to believe than on such facts as are available it may be appropriate to consider the matter in a little detail. Firstly we must try to see the general religious situation of the sixteenth century which was so markedly different from the religious outlook of today. At that time in Western Europe belief in the Christian faith was widespread. There were differences which we shall mention in a moment, but in spite of these the general doctrines of Christendom were accepted without question. Heresy, which was interpreted as a disagreement with established doctrines, usually in matters of detail, was a heinous crime. Second, not only was the Christian faith accepted but also the Bible was taken to be literally true. In consequence where texts of an astronomical or cosmological kind were found these were considered to be truly correct statements. The divine inspiration of scripture was unquestioned. We see then that speculation was constrained within certain limits, imposed from without by religious doctrine. To propose ideas which made nonsense of or differed from the accepted dogmas was not only novel but also dangerous. Thus we can appreciate why Osiander inserted the second preface to *De Revolutionibus*. He realized[1] that while the Christian communities would accept a heliocentric hypothesis as an improved calculating device there would be likely to be trouble if it was thought that the heliocentric view was really a claim for a physically moving Earth. At this time the Roman Catholic Church was clearly willing to consider a less fundamental interpretation, otherwise Copernicus, with his own belief in the reality of the Earth's motion, would never have dedicated his work to Pope Paul III. The Roman Catholic Church was able to demand obedience for wider reasons than purely scriptural and could therefore afford to take a more liberal attitude. On the other hand the Protestant Churches had, in dissenting from Roman domination, to find an authoritative guide and they turned to the Bible as the source of doctrine, behaviour, and Church government. Osiander was a Protestant and therefore would concern himself more with the scriptural significance of the heliocentric theory than would Copernicus. Such texts as

[1] We must be careful here. Osiander *may* really have thought the evidence only strong enough to support a new calculating method and no more. However, it seems likely that whatever his private opinion he inserted the preface because he was motivated by the reasons given; for, after all, it does not seem to have been the wish of Copernicus himself.

those which referred to the stability of the Earth,[1] made it clear that the Copernican doctrines *must* be purely a calculating device. At the present day such a fundamentalist approach may well appear naïve although it must be realized that, even now, there are a very small minority of sects which still take such a view. For the sixteenth century there are certainly extenuating circumstances which should make us temper any stern criticisms of this attitude which we may feel tempted to make. Biblical criticism or, more correctly, a critical approach to scripture is a comparatively new innovation. Moreover, as we have remarked, there was not at the time of the publication of *De Revolutionibus* conclusive observational evidence that the Earth moved in an orbit about the Sun. Observational methods had to be refined before such evidence could be obtained. But above all there was in men's minds the belief that a sojourn on Earth was but a prelude and a training for an eternal life hereafter. To follow doctrines which militated against the faith brought one in danger of eternal damnation instead of eternal bliss and it was clear that they should be avoided. To sum up, then, it was the interpretation of scripture which led to opposition to the doctrines of Copernicus and brought the Protestants out against him; the Roman Catholic Church raised no objections for nearly one hundred years after publication, by which time Protestant objections were less intense.

However, the whole religious outlook, in so far as the heliocentric theory is concerned, became irritated by the work of Giordano Bruno (1548–1600), who was born near Naples and at the age of fourteen entered a Dominican[2] monastery. Bruno was by temperament a rebel. He was also a reckless speaker and was in due course excommunicated. After excommunica-

---

[1] Chronicles 16^{30}; Psalms 93^1, 96^{10}.
[2] The Dominican order was primarily a popular preaching order of great orthodoxy. St Thomas Aquinas was a Dominican, as also were Savonarola and Albertus Magnus.

tion he travelled through Europe, and spent two years in England under the protection of the French ambassador. Bruno was a supporter of the atomist views of Leucippus and Democritus although in so doing he never accepted their thorough-going materialism; he did however strongly favour the neo-Platonic approach and supported the concept of a universal soul – a dangerous heresy in those days. Two of his books, written in England in 1584, were published in Venice so that they would sell better on the Continent; they were *La Cena de la Ceneri* (Ash Wednesday Supper) and *De l'infinito universo e Mondi*. His last work to deal with cosmology, his *De Monade*, was written seven years later. Bruno's books were full of obscurities, *De Monade*, for example, being a blend of prose and poetry, yet they received a wide circulation in Western Europe and clearly exerted much influence. Bruno was brought into contact with the Copernican theory while he was in England, probably through the efforts of Thomas Digges (*d.* 1595), and he became a strong supporter of the heliocentric theory. His books helped to spread this view widely on the Continent. Bruno's approach to scripture is of interest – it was similar to that of Galileo and indeed that adopted by many English Protestants as well as those on the Continent, after the first shock of the heliocentric theory had been absorbed. It considered scripture as divinely inspired as far as its spiritual teaching was concerned, but fallible in matters of natural philosophy – as Galileo expressed it 'The Bible tells us not how the heavens go, but how to go to heaven'. This approach is still found a practical one even in the twentieth century.[1] With this attitude of mind Bruno was able to let his approach to cosmology be as untrammelled by outside influences as possible. He took the universe as infinite in extent and therefore, while he supported the heliocentric theory, he did not place the Sun at the centre of the universe

[1] See, for example, Gore, Goudge and Guillaume, *A New Commentary on Holy Scripture*, London, 1928.

– in his infinite universe there was, of course, no central point. Bruno agreed with the idea of a rotating Earth and in his argument to support this view came close to the principle of inertia; he also suggested that the Sun itself rotated. In discussing the apparently constant appearance of the constellations Bruno suggested that the stars were not fixed but that their distances are so great that their movements cannot be observed. He further suggested that the stars were suns and had planetary systems of their own, and even went so far as to consider the existence of double star systems, and proposed that planets further out from the Sun rotated more quickly on their axes although his reason for this assumption was hardly a physical one – their quicker rotation being necessary to make the nights shorter and so to counteract the lower temperatures they would have due to their great distances from the Sun itself. His belief that they were inhabited supported the argument. Finally, in *De Monade*, Bruno suggested that the Earth's axis would always remain parallel to itself without the application of a special force; this was different to the idea of Copernicus who had proposed a force in order to keep the direction of the axis fixed in space. Bruno was an ingenious and forward-looking speculator on astronomical problems but, correct though many of his ideas later proved to be, it must be realized that they could not be supported by any observational evidence. Bruno was also a heretic. In spite of his excommunication he always hankered after a reconciliation with his Church and was persuaded to return to Venice, from whence he was taken to Rome and tried. After seven years' imprisonment he was finally burned at the stake. It is often said, or at least implied, that his immolation was punishment for the advanced scientific views he proposed. However, it seems that the real reason was because of his heretical religious views. He wrote of these with many polemics, and criticized the Church, which in consequence felt that there was good reason for him to be tried and silenced. Bruno was, then, most likely burned not for his science but for his heresy and religious unorthodoxy. However his religious polemics were pronounced side by side with his astronomical views and these, in consequence, became suspect also. The upshot was a hardening in the attitude of the Roman Catholic Church which, in a few years, classified the Copernican views as heretical and the teaching of his system as anathema.

In England the Church had undergone reformation, and the heliocentric hypothesis was allowed freedom. Robert Recorde (*fl.* 1556) was Court physician, an able Greek scholar and fine mathematician. He was also a pioneer in education, being the first to write textbooks in the vernacular. In 1556 he published his *Castle of Knowledge* in which he made favourable mention of the Copernican theory, while in the same year John Field's *Almanack* contained a preface by the famous Dr Dee who, like Recorde, spoke well of the new heliocentric view. The greatest protagonist of the new views seems, however, to have been Thomas Digges. Stimulated by the appearance in 1572 of a super-nova which was visible in daylight he tried to use this to gain some observational proof of the Copernican hypothesis. Believing that a new star must lie in the Earth's atmosphere he attempted, using the 'fixed' stars as a background and the Earth's diurnal rotation as a base-line equal to the Earth's diameter, to measure the parallax of the super-nova. He was, as we might expect, unsuccessful and he therefore suggested that the star in question was a true star but that its increase in brightness was only apparent, and due to the Earth's orbital motion. He predicted a brightening again twelve months later. This did not occur but this does not seem to have deterred him in his support of the heliocentric system. Indeed in 1576 he published a revised edition of his father's (Leonard Digges) perpetual calendar (the *Prognostication Everlasting*) which, although it gave, as hitherto, a sketch of the Ptolemaic system, contained an appendix on the heliocentric hypothesis, using a translation into the vernacular of part of the first book of *De Revolutionibus*. Moreover, a diagram of the new system was included and here the stars were shown distributed throughout space and not, as was customary, on a sphere. The additional suggestion was also made that the majority of stars are never seen because their immense distances made them appear too dim to be observable. Thomas Digges was a practical man, being muster-master-general of the English forces in the low countries and in charge of the fortifications of Dover, and still seeking proof of the motion of the Earth he arranged to experiment by dropping a weight by the side of the mast of a moving ship. He observed that the weight moved at all times parallel to the mast. The experiment was really evidence of inertia but, in addition, it did serve to show how wrong was Aristotle's argument that if the Earth rotated the stationary air would cause gusts of immense violence. Digges' appendix to the 1576 edition of the *Prognostication Everlasting* had little effect on the Continent for it was, as we have remarked, written in English. However, in England it helped the early synthesis of the heliocentric theory with the idea of infinite space – a cosmological concept of considerable importance.

The Copernican theory was originally accepted primarily because it gave greater ease in computation of planetary positions. The Ptolemaic system had been satisfactory until the increasing number of observations over the years had made it necessary to increase unduly the number of epicycles. With wider agreement to the heliocentric point of view being taken, there was, clearly, a need for more and better observations. It was therefore fortunate that at this time the astronomer Tycho Brahe should have begun his accurate observing. Tycho Brahe was born in 1546 of a noble Swedish family which settled in Denmark. He was interested in astronomy and astrology from an early age but was stimulated into taking matters further when, at the age of seventeen, he observed a conjunction of Jupiter and Saturn and found that the correct date of the phenomenon was not given in any of the tables then available. He travelled widely, and at the age of twenty-four returned to Denmark, firmly resolved to study astronomy and other scientific subjects. He brought back to Denmark with him a large quadrant which he had designed, and he established an alchemical laboratory and observatory at a monastery from which the monks had been driven out and which was then in the possession of his uncle. In November 1572 the super-nova, already mentioned in connexion with Thomas Digges, gave Tycho additional impetus in his astronomical work. Like Digges he tried also to measure its parallax and, likewise, concluded that it lay further away than the Moon, thus making it a truly celestial phenomenon. Tycho also observed carefully the changes in brightness of the star. The year after the super-nova had appeared he published his first book *De Nova Stella*. Thereafter he began his travels again, visiting Wilhelm IV, the Landgrave of Hesse, who was a well-known amateur astronomer and who had an observatory with a rotating roof. King Frederick II of Denmark was keen that Tycho should return to his country and tempted him back from Basle by making over to him the island of Hveen together with ample finance to enable a magnificent observatory to be built. The construction was begun in 1756 and the main building named Uraniborg or 'Castle of the Sky'. The instruments consisted of sextants, quadrants, armillary spheres and clocks of various kinds, while Tycho also had a printing press and a paper mill, as well as an alchemical laboratory and a workshop. He worked here for twenty-one years and prepared sets of astronomical observations of an accuracy never before obtained. Tycho was however a difficult man. He got on badly with the state officials and when, on the death of Frederick II, a military protectorate took over state affairs, there were complaints from the tenants of Hveen, and in 1597 Tycho left the island. After a short period in Germany he finally settled at Prague as court mathematician to the emperor Rudolph II, and he died there in 1601.

Tycho was an acute observer who not only used instruments designed by himself and constructed under his personal supervision, but also appreciated that however well made any instrument was and no matter how accurately it was engraved, it could not be fashioned without having inherent errors. Tycho therefore established the principle, which has been followed ever since, of determining the instrumental errors of his observing equipment and taking these into account in all his observations. The positional accuracy he obtained, using of course open sights, was 4'. Tycho's observations, besides those on the super-nova of 1572, were concerned with the Moon, the planets and comets. In 1577 there appeared a bright naked-eye comet which caused widespread interest on the Continent and gave rise to the publication of many pamphlets. Tycho made careful observations of it and correlated them with those made by others. He was able to prove conclusively that the comet lay further away than the Moon. With the observations by Thomas Digges and Tycho on the super-nova of 1572, by Tycho and others on the comet of 1577, the Greek concept of the immutability of the heavens, together with any ideas which were still entertained as to the physical reality of the crystalline spheres of the planets, were for ever shattered. However, the full implications of these vitally important discoveries took time to make themselves felt. There was much prejudice and lack of proper understanding to be overcome. Yet with time, and the work of men like Kepler and Galileo, a new physics emerged and unlike previous centuries it did not take long to make its effect – within fifty years the cosmological picture was to change in a profound way.

Tycho's work on the Moon and planets brought new factors

ISLAM AND CHRISTENDOM

to light. His lunar observations led him to state in some detail the inequalities of the Moon's orbital motion known as variation[1] and annual equation.[2] As far as the planets were concerned Tycho took the important step of observing them as often as possible, that is to say at as many points in their orbits as possible. While such observations seem obvious to us it must be remembered that the accepted custom was to observe planets only at conjunctions, or other times of unusual interest. In addition Tycho showed that the idea of trepidation, proposed by Tabit-ben-Korra, was false; he carefully established a new value for the rate of precession, as well as compiling a catalogue of 777 stars wherein their positions were compared with the position of the Sun.[3] He also used the celestial equator as a reference circle. This was again an innovation for the previous custom had been to use the ecliptic and to give all co-ordinates in terms of celestial latitude and longitude.[4]

Tycho was a strong Protestant, and was not happy about the Copernican hypothesis because of scriptural texts, to which reference has already been made. However, he appreciated that the Ptolemaic system could no longer be supported, and he therefore set about developing his own system. This was, in effect, a compromise between the geocentric and heliocentric views. Tycho postulated a fixed Earth around which the Moon and, in a larger orbit, the Sun revolved. However, the planets and comets were supposed to orbit around the Sun. The stars he supposed to be fixed to a sphere. In support of his contentions Tycho emphasized that if the Earth moved

---

[1] Variation is discernible as a retardation or acceleration of the Moon's orbital motion.

[2] Annual equation is due to changes in rate caused by changes in the Sun's attractive force and due to alterations in the distances of Earth, Sun and Moon.

[3] Tycho achieved this by using the planet Venus as an intermediate point of reference.

[4] See Appendix V.

stellar parallax should be observable and, after a careful search, he satisfied himself of the absence of this evidence. Thus he could claim that his own system presented a view which both satisfied observation and provided a simple means of computation.

With Tycho we virtually end a major phase in the history of astronomy and cosmology. Here we have seen the last attempt to fit some system of uniform circular motions to account for the motions of the planets. Here too we have observed the destruction of the concept of the changeless nature of the heavenly bodies, a destruction which was to help in changing the entire outlook of astronomers. Tycho the accurate observer, the eccentric who, having lost his nose in a duel, made himself a false one, the scriptural fundamentalist who could not abide the idea of a moving Earth, was the last of a long line of astronomers and philosophers who grappled with the errant planets and systematized their motions by ingenious geometrical explanations based on æsthetic considerations.

Chapter 6

THE NEW APPROACH:
I. DYNAMICS

We come now to the period of the great development of astronomy and cosmology. With the overthrow of the authority of Aristotle and Ptolemy and the ever increasing emphasis placed on accurate observation and experiment, a new phase in men's outlook developed. Full freedom of speculation, unhampered by religious limitations, took many centuries to mature, yet men of many nations were approaching the challenge of the heavens with new ideas and new techniques. We ourselves, in the twentieth century, are not only heirs of this period, but really part of it. Much happened with haste compared to the early developments which have so far been sketched. It is therefore necessary for us to consider the continued developments of astronomy and cosmological speculation in a more piecemeal fashion. We shall have to adopt two main lines of approach. On the one hand the mathematical-theoretical aspects of the problems attacked and sometimes solved will be considered; on the other we shall attend to the differences and developments in observing methods and techniques. These two aspects run side by side, the one influencing the other. Although we must make some artificial division between them, it must be emphasized that any such division is for convenience only. With this in mind we can, then, in this chapter turn to the death pangs of the hypothesis of uniform circular motions and briefly consider the developments of a truly analytical approach to dynamical astronomy.

The first steps in the new direction were taken by Johannes Kepler. Born in Weil der Stadt in Würtemburg, Kepler was a sickly child. However, he obviously had a penetrating mind which developed apace when he entered the university of Tübingen, there to study theology. In the course of this work he read mathematics under Michael Maestlin, and this had a significant effect on him. Maestlin was a supporter of the Copernican hypothesis and it was through him that Kepler first became aware of the heliocentric viewpoint. Moreover, Kepler also came into contact with neo-Platonism and so became concerned, cosmologically, with seeking æsthetically satisfactory arrangements of the planetary system. In the event Kepler gave up his idea of a theological career and decided to devote himself to astronomy. He was certain, in his own mind, that there was a true celestial harmony in the planetary system, and he set himself the task of discovering it. At twenty-two years of age he became a professor at Tübingen, but after a year's work he was driven by religious persecution to Graz. Here, as a provincial surveyor, he seems to have found considerable time for speculation, for two years later, in 1596, his first ideas on the harmony of the solar system saw the light of day in his *Mysterium Cosmographicum*. Copies of the book were sent to Tycho Brahe and Galileo, and earned Kepler a great reputation. After setting forth evidence on behalf of the Copernican theory, Kepler used the main body of the book to enunciate his main thesis which seems, in some ways, to be best described as a sixteenth-century infusion of Greek geometrical thought. Kepler proposed that the distances of the planets from the Sun were directly related to the five regular geometrical solids. Taking the greatest distance (aphelion) of one planet, and the least distance (perihelion) of the next, he obtained a space which could be exactly filled by one of these solids. For example, considering the planets Mercury and Venus, Kepler obtained:

$$\frac{\text{greatest distance of Mercury}}{\text{least distance of Venus}} =$$

$$\frac{\text{radius of sphere inscribed in regular octahedron}}{\text{radius of sphere circumscribed round regular octahedron}}$$

and his scheme, in general, was as follows:

    Mercury
          – octahedron
    Venus
          – icosahedron
    Earth
          – dodecahedron
    Mars
          – tetrahedron
    Jupiter
          – cube
    Saturn

In order to obtain as precise a result as possible, Kepler assumed that the planes of the planetary orbits passed through the centre of the Sun. In this he differed from Copernicus, who had not only taken circular orbits but had also considered them as passing through the centre of the Earth's orbit and not the centre of the Earth itself. Kepler, however, was still unsatisfied, and he sought improved measures of planetary positions.

Having married when in Tübingen, and still being unable to return there because of religious persecution, Kepler accepted, in 1600, the offer of Tycho Brahe to move to Prague and there take up the post of Brahe's assistant. Kepler accepted this offer the more readily in view of Tycho Brahe's fame as an accurate observer. Brahe died in 1601, and Kepler was given the position of court mathematician. Brahe, as we have seen, had his own cosmological system. He handed over to Kepler his observations of the planet

Mars, and expressed a very firm hope that Kepler would find, after carefully examining them, that the Copernican hypothesis was untenable. It was fortunate that the observations were indeed those of Mars; for of all the planets except Mercury, Mars has the most eccentric orbit. Kepler took the observations, and tried fitting an orbit by trial and error. This was a tedious process, and he made upwards of seventy trials. In due course Kepler was led to perceive that the Earth's orbit has an equant like that of any other planet, and, bringing a physical approach to bear on the problem, he suggested that the Sun turned on its axis and that its 'rays' acted like the spokes of a wheel and forced the planets along, the 'virtue' of these rays lying in the plane of the ecliptic. After five solid years' work Kepler became convinced that the only orbital figure which would satisfy the observations was an ellipse, and he was able to enunciate, for Mars, two of his laws of planetary motion – first that the path of the planet was an ellipse with the Sun at one focus, and secondly that the radius vector[1] swept out equal areas in equal times. It will be noted that these two laws express an equivalent to uniform circular motion, at least from the æsthetic point of view. In 1609 he published his *Astronomia Nova*,[2] in which he described his results, his failures and how he came to adopt his laws. He still sought an inner harmony, and ten years later published the *Harmonices Mundi*. In this great work he enunciated his third law, discovered the year before, which stated that, for every planet, the ratio of the square of its sidereal period and the cube of its mean distance from the Sun is constant and equal. The importance of this is obvious, for it means that if the distance from the Sun of any one planet is known then the distances of the other planets can

---

[1] Line joining the centre of the planet and the centre of the Sun.

[2] The full title of the work is significant: *Astronomia Nova seu Physica Cœlestis, tradita commentariis de motibus stellæ Martis Ex observationibus G.V. Tychonis Brahe.*

THE NEW APPROACH: I. DYNAMICS

be obtained, provided, of course, their periods are known.[1] In this book Kepler also proposed a system of harmonies between the angular velocities of the planets and the tempered musical scale.[2] It seems that he did not believe in a real 'harmony of the spheres', but thought that the proposals he made showed a mathematical form of an inner harmony of the universe itself.

Between 1618 and 1621 there also appeared Kepler's *Epitome Astronomiæ Copernicæ*, which was in effect a systematic treatise on astronomy. It was, as its title claims, based on the Copernican outlook. The first 'book' appeared a year before the *Harmonices Mundi*, and extended the first two planetary laws to all the planets, whereas in the *Astronomia Nova* they had been applied only to Mars. The whole work is of special interest, for in it Kepler attempted a physical explanation of his third law of planetary motion and the tides, proposing a 'magnetic' virtue or force between the Sun and the planets, the Earth and the Moon. Moreover, he considered the effects of the approach to each other of bodies in space, and virtually used the concept of 'mass' which was later to become so important.

Kepler was a 'transition' figure. He stands between the ancient world and seventeenth-century dynamics. His approach was truly what we would call scientific. He let the observations lead him wheresoever they might, and expressed his results in mathematical form. His laws were the results of much labour and careful application of inductive reasoning. He was also cautious. He believed the Sun to be the centre of the universe (and there was no good reason then why he should not have done so), but when it came to the

---

[1] These quantities may be expressed as

$$\frac{t_1^2}{a_1^3} = \frac{t_2^2}{a_2^3} = \ldots = \frac{t_n^2}{a_n^2}$$

and hence if we know $t_1, t_2, \ldots t_n$ and a, we can obtain $a_2, a_3 \ldots a_n$.

[2] See Appendix III.

stars he refused to commit himself as to whether they were on a sphere or distributed outwards in space. As an applied mathematician Kepler was in the first rank, and his Rudolphine Tables, dedicated to his patron Rudolph II and published in 1627, were in general use for nearly 100 years. The approach he took set the pattern for those who followed, and looking back on Kepler we can see that, without doubt, a new era had indeed dawned.

In England Kepler's work was supported by Jeremiah Horrox (1617–1641). In spite of his early death at the age of twenty-five, Horrox made some notable contributions. By dint of careful observation he and William Crabtree found errors in published ephemerides, including the Rudolphine Tables. They made corrections; Horrox predicted a transit of Venus in 1639, and he and Crabtree made the first observations of this phenomenon. Their results were summed up by Horrox in his *Venus in Sole visa*, which was published after his death. Horrox's other great contributions were his work, using Kepler's elliptic motions, on the motions of the Moon and his experiments with a conical pendulum bob; he transferred this concept to the Solar System, believing that a rotation of the Sun was necessary in order that the planets might describe their observed elliptical orbits and not merely move to and fro. Although not explicitly stated, we have here again an example of the application of terrestrial physics to the problems of celestial dynamics, an approach which was also utilized by Galileo Galilei (1564[1]–1642) who did much towards the development of physical synthesis of celestial motions.

Galileo was born at Pisa, educated at the Jesuit monastery there, and after leaving the monastery, studied mathematics for two years. He then taught at Pisa,[2] Padua and Florence.

---

[1] Also the date of birth of William Shakespeare.
[2] The legend that Galileo dropped different weights from the leaning tower of Pisa and before an immense crowd is apochryphal. This experi-

THE NEW APPROACH: I. DYNAMICS

In 1597 he received his copy of Kepler's *Mysterium Cosmographicum*, and confessed that he had been a supporter of the heliocentric hypothesis for some time but had feared to make known his views, perhaps because of the fate of Bruno. At Pisa Galileo concerned himself with problems of moving bodies, and followed up the ideas put forward by Benedetti (1530–1590) who had revolted against the Aristotelian physics which was then still generally accepted. Benedetti had continued along the lines of the Paris school of the fourteenth century, and had pursued the concept of impetus, suggesting that projectiles were given an impetus when the process of motion began; this was a very different approach from the Aristotelian, which taught that the motion of a projectile was due to the continued 'pushing' exerted by the air. Galileo extended this work by actual experiment. He set up inclined planes at various angles and allowed small balls of various weights to roll down them; he then measured to what height they ran up an inclined plane opposite. Here Galileo was experimenting with a 'modern' technique; he was concerned only with the weights of moving bodies, the angles of inclination of the planes and the heights reached by the bodies themselves. He had, in fact, designed an experiment to give him the evidence he required for mathematical examination, and he neglected all other irrelevant factors. In the early seventeenth century this kind of approach was indeed an innovation, and, moreover, an innovation of very great importance.

Galileo then applied his results to the behaviour of an 'earthy' body (i.e. a body of like material to that of the Earth, in distinction to the Aristotelian idea that a 'heavenly' body must of necessity be of a different substance which had eternal existence). He considered the question of such a body rotating round the centre of the universe, seeking an answer

---

ment was carried out earlier by Stevinus (1548–1620) and John Grotius. Galileo *may* have repeated the experiment, but certainly not before a large crowd.

to the problem of whether, under a central attraction, such a body would continue its motion for ever; but he was unable to find a definite answer. To state this is in no way to disparage his efforts. For a solution to be obtained a radically new approach to the question of motion was required; and although Galileo made some moves in this direction, it was Newton who produced a new synthesis embracing both celestial and terrestrial phenomena.

Galileo's other contributions to dynamical astronomy came from his observations with the newly-invented telescope. His observations of the Sun showed that this heavenly body underwent changes; his observations of Jupiter showed here a planet which was attended by smaller planetary bodies or satellites which accompanied it on its journey through space; his observations of Venus showed that, like the Moon, this planet presented phases, while his observations of the Moon itself showed up irregularities on its surface and what appeared to be seas. Thus Galileo demonstrated that change occurred on heavenly bodies; he showed the similarity of the Moon to the Earth and to Venus from a physical point of view, and, in Jupiter, another centre of motion in the universe; all these provided observational evidence against the whole Aristotelian outlook. Moreover, he saw that in the telescope stars appeared purely as points of light and so were obviously very far away, and somewhat vitiated the argument that lack of stellar parallax showed the Copernican hypothesis to be untrue. It is no wonder then that his conclusions were met with incredulity and hostility. Men do not take easily to having their generally accepted ideas and syntheses upset, and become obstinate and bitter if the new approach militates against religious doctrines. The telescopic discoveries were announced by Galileo in his *Siderius Nuncius* (1610), and six years later he was summoned before the Inquisition. He was accused of unorthodoxy, for, as was remarked in the previous chapter, he took a modernistic and

THE NEW APPROACH: I. DYNAMICS

non-fundamentalist approach to scripture. Galileo cleared himself of the charge against him, but was warned not to teach or to defend the Copernican doctrines. Nevertheless, he was not put off. He had been working for some time on a book in which the Copernican and Ptolemaic systems were to be discussed, and in 1632 this was published under the title *Dialogo sopra i due massimi sistemi del Mondo, Tolemaico e Copernico*. This volume was written for the intelligent public at large, and as the title states, was in the form of a dialogue. Three characters – Salviati, who speaks the views of Galileo, Sagredo, a man with an open mind, and Simplicio, who supports the Ptolemaic/Aristotelian outlook – argue the matter. Their discussion is divided into four 'days'; on the first the question of the Earth as centre of the universe is considered, on the second the Earth's diurnal rotation, the orbital motion of the Earth on the third, and on the fourth and final day the question of the tides. The book was carefully worded; although the Copernican theory was victorious, it was not decisively so, and the book passed the censor. But soon troubles began, ending with Galileo being put on trial for disobeying the Inquisition's previous injunction. As is well known, Galileo retracted his statement – but not under torture, as is sometimes stated, and he was finally permitted to retire to a farm in Arcetri, Florence, where he remained under 'house arrest' to the end of his life. Difficulties were not however at an end, for, forbidden to concern himself further with cosmology, Galileo took up again his studies on the 'science of motion', and in 1638 his *Discorsi e Dimonstrazioni Matematiche intorno à due Nuove Science attenti alle Meccanica & i Movimenti Locali* was published in Holland, the manuscript of which, Galileo claimed, had been 'stolen'!

The first two great protagonists of the new dynamical astronomy worked under difficulties. Galileo fell foul of the Roman Catholic Church, and Kepler was driven out of his country to Prague. The new philosophical outlook was then generally beset by religious bigotry, although it is only fair to state that in England the Copernican and Keplerian ideas were studied freely and a translation of Galileo's *Dialogo* was published in 1661 by Thomas Salusbury. Horrox and Crabtree openly took the ideas of Kepler and worked on them. However, the new philosophy was beginning to get under way, and there was, in fact, no going back. As had happened before in connexion with Greek ideas, the seventeenth-century cosmological theories became absorbed into Christian orthodoxy; but fortunately for freedom of speculation, they never again became synonymous with it.

In spite of difficulties, work on the Continent continued, and the need for a broad synthesis became apparent. The first great attempt was made by René Descartes (1596–1650) who made a bold bid to find an all-embracing system of natural knowledge. Descartes was born in The Hague and educated at a Jesuit school. Having campaigned with the army, he suddenly turned to philosophy at the age of twenty-four, and retired to Holland, where he worked on his ideas for two decades. Descartes finally travelled to Sweden, where he became royal tutor, and died there at the age of fifty-five. Early on Descartes accepted the Copernican view, and in 1634 produced a tract on cosmology which, however, he felt it expedient to keep unpublished because of the Inquisition's treatment of Galileo and the hardening attitude of the Roman Catholic Church. The work was not, in fact, published until 1664, fourteen years after his death, under the title *Le Monde*. Nevertheless he allowed his cosmological views to be made public in 1644 with the publication of the *Principia Philosophiæ*, in which he phrased matters carefully so that no offence could be taken. The *Principia Philosophiæ* was divided into three parts. In the first Descartes began with his basic tenet 'cogito ergo sum' ('I think, therefore I am')[1] from which

[1] This he had previously announced in his *Discours de la Méthode*, 1637.

basis of certainty he built his philosophical edifice. Parts two and three are concerned with his cosmological speculation. He put forward the concepts of extended substance and thinking substance. As it is not possible to think of a limit to space, it must, he argued, be infinite; and again, since it is possible to think of dividing material particles without cessation, there could not be 'atoms'. Extended substance fills space and is continually moving, but, Descartes taught, it was all of one kind, and its qualities other than movement were merely shown us by our senses. He suggested that the amount of motion of this extended substance is proportional to the product of the quantity of matter and its velocity. In other words, Descartes gave a definition of momentum. He also formulated the law of inertia, by claiming that a body always moves in the same direction with the same speed indefinitely, provided it meets with no collision. With these basic ideas he went on, in part three, to claim that the universe must, therefore, be in the form we find it. This form, Descartes claimed, is of a space filled with matter of various sizes in continual circulation and at differing velocities. Following on this theory of vortices, he proposed that fire accumulates at the centre of each vortex, the result being the formation of stars which, taking up the rotation which the vortex possesses, gain an outward pressure. A skin then forms over them, their emission of light ceases, and the vortex collapses. The star then becomes a planet, and at a later date, the planet becomes a satellite – unless, he conjectured, the material is too great in quantity, when the degraded star wanders from vortex to vortex and becomes, therefore, a comet. The satellites observed with the newly-discovered telescope had been, in Descartes' opinion, planets when the present planets were originally stars. The Earth was stationary with respect to its surrounding matter, and carried along with it, the surrounding matter thrusting heavy bodies towards the centre of the Earth. This then was Descartes' general picture.

It was nothing if not ingenious, and indeed was a brilliant construction of the mind. Above all it gave the first physical synthesis of things celestial and terrestrial. Descartes' views had a great vogue, and were studied widely; Newton was taught them at Cambridge, and it was only when his own mathematical approach and gravitational synthesis was propounded that they receded into the limbo of productive, but dated, hypotheses.[1]

The physical approach to celestial problems was continued by Giovanni Borelli (1608–1669). Borelli was concerned with the reason for the rotation of the planets, and studied the satellite system of Jupiter in order to obtain a clue. He rejected the Keplerian idea of spokes or rays from a rotating Sun in view of the lack of evidence, and also the hypothesis that the planets floated in an extended solar atmosphere. Instead he suggested that orbital motions were compounded of three factors – an 'appetite' of the planet directly towards the Sun, a tangential force, and a natural tendency of the planet to recede from the Sun, that is to say a centrifugal force. The balance between the planet's appetite for the Sun and its tendency to recede from it kept the planet in its orbit, while the tangential force caused its rotation. Borelli then went on to suggest that the planetary system was in equilibrium but, believing that such a system must oscillate about a mean point if it were to remain in equilibrium, he was able to propose that the final form of the orbits must, then, be ellipses. Thus again we can see the new approach in action. Borelli, like Descartes, was hunting for some over-riding systematization. Descartes thought he had discovered it in his vortex theory, and certainly this was a concept which stimulated others and bore much fruit – but which, nevertheless,

[1] It should be remembered that to Descartes we owe the analytical method of specifying the positions and relationship of points, lines and plane figures with reference to co-ordinate axes. This Cartesian geometry was, and still is, a powerful mathematical technique which has been much developed with very fruitful results.

did not give a close enough agreement to observation to satisfy completely the hunt for a final solution of the problem of planetary motion. Borelli's ideas on the forces causing planetary motions show a very sophisticated approach. Yet here again there was obviously a need for a more taut explanation of the attractive forces operating, so that not only general planetary behaviour but also the various irregularities of planetary motion could be accounted for. This need was realized even if it was not overtly expressed.

In England a number of philosophers were concerning themselves with the problems of planetary motions. At first they used to meet for informal discussions in taverns and coffee-houses, and were in the practice of conducting experiments and reporting their results to one another. This desire to discuss with others one's own efforts, ideas and experiments showed a very different approach to that of a short time before, when philosophers had tended to work in isolation or with their own 'disciples' and keep their knowledge from the gaze of the vulgar. Moreover, the increasing popularity of an exchange of views was influenced no doubt by the suggestions of Francis Bacon (1561–1626) who put forward the idea that if enough experiments were done and the results collated, then all natural knowledge would be discovered. Such an outlook is not satisfactory in practice; the inductive method of reasoning, where the general is developed from the particular, provides the only real method of progress. However, Bacon certainly emphasized the experimental approach, and stimulated those interested in the 'new' philosophy to discuss their problems together and even to form themselves into a society or club. He was, as he himself said, 'the bell which calls the wits together'. In 1660 there was formed in London the Royal Society, which,[1] in 1662, received its first Royal Charter from Charles II. At the present

---

[1] The full title is 'Royal Society of London for Improving Natural Knowledge'.

day it is the oldest and leading scientific society in the world, and in the seventeenth century it provided much stimulus to the new philosophy as well as a forum for discussion and experiment. Those who were specially concerned with the problem of what forces operated to cause the planets to behave according to Kepler's laws were all members, or became so after they began their research work. The architect Sir Christopher Wren, who had previously been professor of astronomy at Oxford, together with Edmond Halley and Robert Hooke often had occasion to discuss planetary motions, and they were not the only ones who believed that some kind of inverse square law would provide a solution. Indeed on one occasion, when Wren had offered a prize for whoever should be able to solve the problem, Hooke claimed that he had obtained a mathematical proof of the validity for planetary motions of such a law, but in the event he never produced the answer. Halley, however, knowing Isaac Newton and his great abilities as a mathematician and physicist, visited Cambridge and learned from Newton that he had come to such a solution and obtained a proof. Newton was unable to find his results, and promised to re-compute the matter and send the results to Halley. The results arrived, and for the first time the planetary problem was provided with a solution of unparalleled completeness and perfection.

Newton himself was in some ways a recluse. He detested the pettiness which so often arose over matters of priority of discovery; he intensely disliked wrangling over arguments concerning hypotheses, and was for ever insisting on testing by experiment. Isaac Newton was born in 1642. He went as a sizar or poor scholar to Cambridge in 1661. At the time of the great plague in 1666, when the University was closed, he returned to Woolsthorpe in Lincolnshire and it was here that his early work on gravitation was carried out. Newton was first of all concerned with the nature of the force which kept the Moon in its orbit, and set himself four questions by answering which he thought he could solve the problem. First, he attempted to determine the variation of this force, called gravity,[1] with distance from the Earth; secondly to calculate, on such law of variation as might be taken, the Earth's gravity at the distance of the Moon; thirdly, assuming as a first approximation, that the Moon's orbit is circular, Newton wanted to find the acceleration due to gravity which a body at the distance of the Moon would undergo. Fourthly, and finally, the law of acceleration and the actual acceleration observed had to be compared. For the law of variation of gravity with distance Newton studied the planetary orbits, and using Kepler's laws he found that the variation of the force was indeed inversely proportional to the square of the distance. Assuming this variation to hold for the Earth as well as the Sun, he then applied the law to a body at the Moon's distance and compared this to a body at the Earth's surface. Finally, then, after considering the actual motions concerned, he found that 'the results answer pretty nearly'. In 1685, nearly twenty years later, he was able to complete his work by making certain that the gravitational force of a body was as if 'concentrated' at the centre of the body. Newton's work and results were published in 1687 in what is, clearly, one of the greatest works of science that has ever seen the light of day, his *Principia mathematica philosophiæ naturalis*. The *Principia* went through many vicissitudes before publication, and Newton more than once relinquished the task because of his wish to withdraw from the strife which arose over misunderstandings or disagreements with his advanced ideas. To Halley must go the credit for nursing the book through the press, and its distinguished author through the rough seas of petty criticism.

Newton's masterpiece set out the principles of dynamics

[1] The term 'gravity' was in common use at the time when Newton carried out his work.

and dynamical astronomy in a way never previously envisaged, let alone attempted. At one blow not only was the mystery of planetary motion provided with a solution, but also under one powerful and exact physical law the whole gamut of terrestrial and celestial motion was gathered into one brilliant correlation. So great was the influence of Newton's work on future astronomy and cosmology, as well as in other fields of physical science, that we must pause for a few moments to describe some of the concepts which he propounded so clearly and handled with such consummate ability. Other able minds had been working on the problems discussed in the *Principia*, but it is the clear-sightedness which he brought to bear which allowed him to make his great synthesis. As he himself wrote,[1] 'If I have seen further it is by standing on the shoulders of giants.' Of all men Newton was certainly under no illusions on this score, but he had a clarity of thought which can only cause us even now to see that Halley's description[2] of the *Principia* as a 'divine treatise' was hardly an exaggeration. The book opens with a definition of the concepts of mass, momentum and force, after which Newton's three laws of motion are enunciated. These laws of motion are important not only for the influence they exerted, but also because for the first time in history it was proposed that a body could either be in a *state* of motion or rest, whereas hitherto motion had always been considered as a special (and temporary) condition of a body. This is shown clearly in his first 'law' – a body removed from all other bodies would continue in a state of rest or uniform motion in a straight line – and, of course, means that a moving body must be acted upon by an external force or by forces if its motion is to cease or be other than in a straight line. Such a definition made it impossible any longer to consider the

[1] In a letter dated 5 February 1676 written to Robert Hooke.
[2] Halley in a letter to Newton dated 5 April 1687 reporting the completion of the printing of the work.

elliptical motion of the planets as due to something inherent in their nature; it required that external forces must be postulated to account for their particular motion. In his second 'law' Newton therefore went on to state that a change of motion (i.e. rate of change of momentum) is proportional to the force acting on a body, and takes place in the direction of this force; he then completed his thesis by the 'third law' in which it is stated that action and reaction are equal (i.e. if body A pulls body B, then B pulls A by an equal amount). With these definitions Newton treats in 'Book' I of motion through a non-resisting medium. Here, using the inverse square law of attraction, Newton *proved* that bodies acting under it alone would describe Keplerian orbits. It was the proof of this which had foiled Hooke, Halley, Wren and others. In this first Book, Newton also discussed the attraction of a homogeneous sphere about a point, and also of the force existing between two spheres both of which are thus attracted. This latter question, involving, in fact, the behaviour of three bodies, has not even now received a general solution, but Newton took a particular instance, namely the Sun–Earth–Moon system, where of course one can consider one of the three bodies, the Moon, as being under the influence of the Earth only due to the immense distance of the Sun. He obtained from this consideration the inequalities of the Moon's motion which had already been found observationally.

In the second section or 'Book', Newton discussed the motion of bodies in resisting media, and disproved, by mathematical reasoning, the tenability of Descartes' vortex hypothesis. The third and last 'Book' is concerned with the enunciation of the principle of universal gravitation. Beginning with the gravitation of the Earth, Newton first showed how our planet must have an ellipsoidal shape due to its axial rotation and how, with such a shape, the phenomenon of precession must necessarily follow. The concept of gravitation was next applied to cometary paths, and Newton showed how a comet's perihelion passage must be a path which is a conic section. From applying gravitation to comets, Newton went on to generalize the concept and thus enunciated his law of universal gravitation in which he proposed that all bodies attract each other with a force which is directly proportional to the product of their masses and inversely proportional to the square of the distance between the bodies.[1]

Moreover, Newton pointed out that, applied to the Solar System, this meant that not only does the Sun attract every planet, but that each planet attracts the Sun; and as the Sun must therefore be subject to many differing pulls, the direction and magnitude of which are continually varying, it was no longer proper to consider the Sun as stationary in the centre of the universe. However, he also appreciated that while the stationary point for the Solar System was the centre of gravity or mass centre of the sun-planet system, this point must in fact be close to the Sun's centre, and would never lie outside the Sun's 'surface'. In this third 'Book' Newton also tackled the problem of the tides. He was able to point out that a tidal force could be used to explain the reason why the Moon always presents the same face to the Earth, the explanation being that this force had slowed down an original axial rotation of the Moon until this was a minimum, that is to say when this period was equal to its orbital period. Newton was however unable to reach any general form of tidal theory.

From this sketch of the ground covered by the *Principia* it will be clear that with its publication, a logical mathematical system based, really, on four basic premises (the three laws of motion and the law of universal gravitation) had

---

[1] Expressed mathematically $F = \dfrac{m_1 m_2}{d^2}$ where m_1, m_2, are the masses of the bodies and d the distance between them (or more precisely between their 'centres of gravity').

been developed which placed all celestial and, indeed, all terrestrial motion on the same footing. Thus the various piecemeal explanations of this or that celestial behaviour which had been offered previously were now correlated under one quantitative umbrella. Moreover, as we shall see, the power of the new methods which he had synthesized was greater than probably he and certainly others ever envisaged. As might be expected, Newton's proposal of universal gravitation was not accepted everywhere without argument, and most wanted to know *what* exactly was the *nature* of the gravitational force. Newton tried to avoid this issue, and pointed out that gravitation was a universal force acting throughout space. There were however those who were of the opinion that for such a force to operate there must be physical contact, even if *via* a universal medium of some kind.

Bentley, then Master of Trinity College, Cambridge, was adamant over queries of this kind, but in a letter written in 1693 Newton answered his critic. Unfortunately the letter was not published until 1756, and confusion over these issues continued. Newton became drawn into the controversies, much though he wished to avoid doing so, and he made some discussion on the hypothesis of an æther which he had already considered in correspondence with Hooke and others before the *Principia* had been written. The æther was supposed to be insusceptible to measurement, and, according to Newton, to become rarefied near solid bodies. It thus could be considered as providing a thrust on a body as the æther 'tried to even itself out'. But fundamentally Newton preferred the idea that gravity was an active 'principle' which operated in the universe, and to leave the question of the nature of gravitation in abeyance.

The general acceptance of universal gravitation came through independent confirmation of the principles which Newton had enunciated. The first to secure such confirmation was Edmond Halley. Halley followed up Newton's work on comets, and, examining the paths at perihelion of the comets of 1531, 1607 and 1682, concluded that these were appearances of the same body. Using the methods given by Newton, Halley worked out an elliptic orbit for the comet, and finding a period of about 76 years suggested that the comet would reappear in 1758.

In December 1758 the comet was observed as Halley had 'predicted', and was therefore known as 'Halley's' comet. This was an important step forward. Comets had always been something of a mystery, and here at last was theory and observation removing them from the realms of the unknown and not understood, and placing them among the natural phenomena of the universe. Yet although we see Halley here providing the first independent confirmation of Newtonian principles, it must be appreciated that observation was only able to clinch the matter some seventy years after the publication of the *Principia* and when both Halley and Newton were dead.

After the advent of Newtonian dynamics the next step forward was taken by James Bradley (1693–1762) who became the third holder of the position of Astronomer Royal.[1] Bradley sought, as many had before him and were to do after, evidence for a parallactic shift of the nearer stars against the background of those more distant. Such a phenomenon was, as we have already remarked, to be expected if the Earth moved round the Sun. After the work of Kepler and Newton there was no doubt about the Earth's motion, but still there was no observational proof. A parallactic shift was not however observed by Bradley, but in the course of his investigations he found that the star γ Draconis, in which he was particularly interested for reasons which we shall consider in the next chapter, deviated by $2''$ per year from its 'true' position, and that this deviation had a 19-year

---

[1] The establishment of the Royal Observatory at Greenwich and the office of Astronomer Royal will be considered in Chapter 7.

period. This was discovered to hold also for other stars, and could be accounted for by a nodding or *nutation* of the Earth's axis. The cause of such nutation was found by d'Alembert (1717–1783) to be due to the attraction of the Moon on the Earth's equatorial bulge, and was completely amenable to Newton's dynamic.[1] This again then was a confirmation of Newton's ideas, which was strengthened not only by this work of d'Alembert but also by his further researches into lunar theory, and by the work of Clairaut (1713–1765) who also tackled the difficult problems of the Moon's orbital motion, and calculated the effects of the attractions or perturbations which the planets Jupiter and Saturn would cause to the orbit of Halley's comet, confirming Halley's own prediction. Mention must also be made of Euler (1707–1783) who also spent some time on studies of the Moon's motion according to Newtonian principles, and in 1753 published tables of the Moon's motion (*Novæ Tabulæ Motuum Solis et Lunæ*) and a treatise on lunar theory (*Theoria Motus Lunæ*). Thus we see that the quantitative foundations which Newton had laid provided an impetus to a mathematical approach to celestial problems, and received continual confirmation by

[1] The centre of attraction of a spherical body lies at its centre. However, the Earth has an equatorial bulge and may, therefore, be considered as a sphere surrounded by a ring of material of similar density. The centre of attraction of the Earth on the Moon does not, therefore, lie at the centre of the Earth. Both the Sun and the Moon attract this ring, the former pulling it into the plane of the ecliptic and the latter into the plane of the lunar orbit. Because the lunar orbit is only inclined at a little more than 5° to the ecliptic both forces tend to combine but, as the Moon is so much nearer than the Sun, its effect is the greater. The result of these forces is to cause precession.

These two forces are not, however, constant in their effect. When the Sun passes across the equator (at equinox), its disturbing force is zero. Likewise when the Moon crosses the equator, its disturbing force is zero – this occurs twice a month. The disturbing forces of both Sun and Moon vary. In addition, because the Moon's orbit also changes its position continually with respect to the ecliptic, the force due to the Moon undergoes more changes than that due to the Sun. The result is seen as a nodding or *nutation* of the Earth's polar axis.

providing theoretical refinements which were required as observational accuracy also increased. Euler did not confine himself only to lunar theory, but also gave a general discussion of planetary motion based on gravitational theory.

However, in spite of all this work, some discrepancies between observational and gravitational theory still remained. There were still non-uniformities to be accounted for, and two mathematicians, Lagrange (1736–1813) and Laplace (1749–1827), finally placed the gravitational theory on an apparently unassailable pedestal. Joseph Lagrange worked for a time under Euler in 1764, winning the prize which the Académie des Sciences in Paris had offered for a mathematical solution to the problem of the Moon's libration. Lagrange developed new methods for tackling the problem, and continued to develop his ideas, tackling next the dynamics of the satellites of Jupiter. Euler had been concerned with the question of the mean distances of the planets and the perturbations caused by the comparatively large masses of Jupiter and Saturn. He had surmised that over a considerable period these perturbations could be considered to average out, but the trouble was to prove that this was so. It was Lagrange who was able to deduce proof, and to show that all the various perturbations to which the planets are subject are, in fact, periodic. Hence it became clear that the Solar System had the possibility of existing for all time, at least from the point of view of the internal forces which were operating. Lagrange's researches and his mathematical developments of the theory of universal gravitation were published in his elegant *Mécanique Analytique*, in which he concerned himself with the principle of the conservation of energy, using the concepts of virtual velocities and least action.

Pierre Laplace also worked on the question of the mean distances of the planets and the satellites of Jupiter. His work on the latter enabled him to apply certain factors to lunar theory and provide an explanation of the acceleration of the Moon's mean motion which had not seemed amenable to Newtonian dynamics. His work in this field led to wide appreciation of new concepts in the general gravitational theory, and was published first in his *Mécanique céleste*. Later, with other researches which he had made, it was published under the direction of the French government, in seven volumes entitled *Œuvres de Laplace*. The first five volumes deal with problems of celestial mechanics – methods of calculation of the motion of the planets and tidal theory, precession, libration of the Moon, the shape and rotation of Saturn's rings, and irregularities and perturbations of planetary motion. Laplace also spent much time on the very difficult problem of a rotating fluid mass, and he considered the aggregation of material by such a mass and the effects of its subsequent cooling. He finally proved that such a mass would assume the form of an ellipsoid of revolution, and went on, as we shall see in due course, to propose a theory about the origin and formation of the Solar System.

All this mathematical work of Euler, d'Alembert, Clairaut, Lagrange and Laplace shows a new approach. It followed on the 'tradition' of Newton, and while mathematical methods had been used, as we have seen, from Babylonian times, in the eighteenth century an application and development of algebraic analysis together with the powerful methods of the calculus, brought a new tool forward for the investigation of the problems of astronomy. The question of celestial motions was given a precision of examination and expression never before available. This was necessary, in view of the increasing precision in observation, and brought terrestrial physical phenomena and celestial motions together in a form that, subconsciously at least, made way for the development of astrophysics, a subject in which physical phenomena of the laboratory and of the stars themselves were tied together, and which we shall consider in the next chapter. Moreover, with

Laplace, the wider question of cosmological origins was approached, for the first time, in a truly mathematical manner. Yet before this mathematical approach was made, the seventeenth century produced some other general ideas which, clearly, were stimulated by the general and widely-embracing nature of Newton's work.

The first bold attempt at a general post-Newtonian cosmology was made by a native of Durham, Thomas Wright (1711–1786), who took the structure of the universe as his problem. Wright was a teacher of mathematics and navigation, and a practical observer. In 1750 he published a *New Hypothesis of the Universe*. Starting from observations of the Milky Way, Wright proposed that the stars were not distributed at random, but believed that they were limited in certain directions. This led to his suggestion that the stellar system was in the form of a disk of infinite radius, and also to the bold idea that the Solar System was situated eccentrically in that part which could at that time be observed. Wright knew of the existence of nebulæ and he considered all of these objects to be external to his thin disk of stars. Considering the meagre observational evidence available in the mid-eighteenth century the proposals of Thomas Wright were bold and brilliant to a degree and, in view of recent developments in cosmology, it is perhaps fitting that the first of the 'new' cosmologists should have been an Englishman. Wright's *New Hypothesis* was read by Immanuel Kant (1724–1804) among others, and without doubt had an influence on this German philosopher's thinking so far as astronomy was concerned. Five years after the appearance of the *New Hypothesis*, Kant produced his own cosmological speculations under the title *Allgemeine Naturgeschichte und Theorie des Himmels*. The work was divided into two parts. The first provided proposals similar to those of Thomas Wright, but in the second part Kant was concerned with the mechanical origin of the universe according to Newtonian principles.

THE NEW APPROACH: I. DYNAMICS

Kant proposed that at first there was a haphazard movement of particles which, under gravitational attraction and some repulsion of the kind discernible in an expanding gas, formed into separate systems. Within these systems Kant realized that there would be continuous collisions of particles which he believed, erroneously, would lead to rotation. Finally, then, he concluded that there were many stellar systems and suggested that the nebulæ were examples of such separate units. All were in rotation. This was a significant step forward, at least as an approach to the problem. It was taken up in greater detail, using mathematical analysis, by Laplace.

However, it must be mentioned that Auguste Comte, a philosopher who was much influenced by Kant, pointed out that correct though Kant's hypothesis might be, there was a limitation in the knowledge man could gain about the nature of the stars. As he could never reach them he could, therefore, never know of what they were made. In the next century Comte was to be proved wrong when new techniques were developed and used. Although he could have no knowledge of such techniques, it is valid to criticize such a state of mind whereby a philosopher could be so foolhardy as to state with such definiteness what would always be the nature of observational limitations. The important point of our criticism is, of course, that there is an important lesson to be drawn from it – namely that whenever we are tempted to set a limit to man's powers or techniques of obtaining knowledge of the physical universe, we must at least qualify our statements. After all we are always limited by the breadth of our outlook and the scientific 'climate' of the day and so often fail to appreciate that entirely new and undreamed of ideas may radically alter the situation.

Kant's *Theorie des Himmels* was followed, in 1761, by publication of the *Cosmological Letters* of Johannes Lambert (1728–1777). Lambert seems to have been unaware of the work of either Wright or Kant but, again from studies of the

Milky Way, he was able to give a description of the universe very like Wright's. He paid particular attention to apparent irregularities in the observed distribution of the stars of the Milky Way. He proposed that there were many stellar systems, of which the Sun and local stars formed one, and he further suggested that all were rotating round a common centre. Thus a general picture of separate stellar systems, all in rotation, was being built up. In addition, the Sun was firmly dethroned from the centre of the universe due to the acceptance of a space of infinite extent, and was beginning to take its place among the general body of stars. Sir William Herschel (1738–1822) added to the observational evidence and also had his own views on stellar distribution. He believed that the stars were uniformly distributed, that is to say that the number of stars per unit volume of space was constant although, after he had observed the existence of a number of star clusters, he modified his opinion.

Observational evidence was being amassed and, with increasingly powerful mathematical techniques coming into use, we can say that both observation and analysis lifted cosmology out of the realms of pure speculation. Mention has already been made of Laplace's interest in the origin of the Solar System and of the publication of the *Œuvres*. In the sixth volume of the latter there was included Laplace's *Exposition du système du monde*, in which his cosmological proposals were given. He began with a rotating mass of gas, rotating, be it noted, *ex hypothesi* and not due to collisions of particles as proposed by Kant. Laplace then calculated that this rotating mass of gas would break up and what was hitherto a rotating ellipsoid would form into a spherical mass with a ring of material around it and lying in the equatorial plane. Laplace next supposed that this ring of material would be unstable and would itself break up, forming the planets, the central mass itself forming the Sun. In brief, then, Laplace proposed the formation of the Solar System from a gaseous nebula, and this nebular hypothesis became, in the nineteenth century, the generally accepted explanation.

Besides the problems of the cosmos on a large scale, there was also the question of its actual size. As far as the Solar System was concerned Kepler's third law gave the relative sizes of the planetary orbits, but the actual scale could not be ascertained until one distance was known in miles, as was pointed out on page 100. Various suggestions were made as to the most satisfactory way of determining the distance from Earth to Sun from which, clearly, the remainder of the planetary distances could be obtained. Laplace appreciated that the question could be solved by gravitational means, using measures of the Earth's perturbations on the Moon and the planets. He computed the result, and obtained, in 1787, a distance of 95 million miles for the mean distance of the Sun. Refinements came in the latter part of the nineteenth century with the development of observational techniques to which we must now turn, for in the nineteenth century it was also in the observational field that cosmology was advanced.

Chapter 7

THE NEW APPROACH:
II. OBSERVATION

The great step in astronomy which occurred at the beginning of the 'modern' period, that is to say the seventeenth century, was the discovery and introduction of the telescope. It is perhaps difficult for us, in the twentieth century, to appreciate the significance of this new tool to astronomers. All through the previous history of the science there was a natural limit to the observational accuracy which could be obtained, however accurate the instruments or however well one took into account, like Tycho Brahe, the inherent errors of the instruments themselves. This was because there is a limit[1] to the resolving power of the human eye, and hence to the finesse with which a star's position can be estimated. However, more significant, initially, was the power to see distant objects which the telescope brought to astronomers, and which made it possible at last to study individual planets and other objects in detail. Much was to arise, then, from the employment of the telescope, and it is no exaggeration to say that the face of astronomy was entirely changed. The date of the discovery of the telescope is uncertain. Leonard Digges, the father of Thomas Digges, claimed to have invented the instrument, while Thomas Harriott (1560–1621) certainly had

[1] The resolving power, or power to separate objects which appear close together, of the human eye is 2′, while that of a telescope is given by a formula, due to William Dawes, $R = \dfrac{4\cdot 5''}{a}$, where R is the resolving power in seconds of arc and a is the aperture of the object-glass or mirror in inches.

a telescope, and has also been credited with the invention. But pride of place is usually given to the spectacle-maker Hans Lippershey, of Middelburg, Holland, who in 1608 certainly filed a patent for such a device. Legend has it that Lippershey's discovery was accidental. Whatever the truth or falsity of the story, the fact remains that the telescope arrived, and in 1609 was put by Galileo to astronomical use. Galileo designed his own instruments, and used a bi-convex object-glass and an eyepiece which was bi-concave. This provided only a small field of view, but Kepler also designed a telescope in which a bi-convex lens was used as an eyepiece, and this was an improvement. Such instruments suffered from both chromatic and spherical aberrations, and to reduce these errors a method of construction using many lenses, and giving the telescope a long total focal length, was adopted. Telescopes of this sort were unwieldy; yet in spite of the development of a different type of instrument by Newton, Gregory and Cassegrain, the long-focus instruments continued in use until, in the eighteenth century, a new development enabled the refractor to be reduced in size with, at the same time, the inherent aberrations considerably reduced. Thus in the early eighteenth century Bradley was still using an instrument of 212 feet focal length. Such 'aerial' telescopes consisted of a wooden beam upon which the lenses were mounted. The beam itself was suspended from a vertical pole by ropes. Thus the instrument cannot have been easy to manipulate; and as only the centre parts of the lenses were put to use, a very careful technique indeed must have been required.

However, at an early stage, the telescope also became accepted as a means of obtaining greater positional accuracy, and instruments of small focal length were constructed and fitted to mural arcs. Moreover, the transit instrument, invented by Olaus Römer (1614–1710), which is virtually a telescope accurately positioned so that its field of view lies due north and south, came to be widely used. The superiority of the telescope as a measuring instrument was not accepted everywhere, and soon after its introduction there arose a notable controversy between Robert Hooke and Johannes Hevelius. Hevelius was an observer of international repute who stuck doggedly to the use of open sights, and refused to be convinced of the superiority of the telescope. In his defence it must be pointed out that he was an observer with exceptional acuity of vision and, moreover, his protagonist Hooke was not the most tactful of men. However, even the diplomatic Halley, who at the age of twenty-three visited Hevelius in Danzig and took with him a sextant fitted with telescopic sights, was unable to convince the older man. The meeting was amicable, but Hevelius still preferred his open sights and used a telescope for general observations only. Nevertheless, the telescopic sight gradually supplanted the open sight. The Keplerian form of telescope was used because the real image formed therein allowed measuring instruments, such as the micrometer, to be attached to the eye-end of the telescope.[1] William Gascoigne (1612–1644), Francesco Generini, and Geminiano Montanari (1633–1687) all introduced forms of the micrometer at about the same time, and these became widely used – especially at the Paris Observatory, while Römer, who was working at Paris, introduced a form of equatorial mounting for the telescope, thus enabling the rotation of the Earth to be taken care of by a movement in one direction only.

It will be clear that the advent of the telescope brought a new impetus into astronomy, and, moreover, a new impetus to the study of light and optics. Newton, and James Gregory (1638–1675) considered the aberrations of the refracting

[1] In the Keplerian telescope the eyepiece, being of convex lens construction, is placed behind the focal plane of the object-glass. Into this focal plane may be placed cross-wires, the wires of a micrometer and similar measuring devices. In the Galilean telescope, the concave nature of the eyepiece necessitates its positioning in front of the focal plane of the object-glass; the image formed by the object-glass is therefore virtual only, and there is nowhere for cross-wires to go.

THE NEW APPROACH: II. OBSERVATION

telescope, and Gregory put forward the opinion that the one way to overcome spherical aberration was for lenses to be figured so that their surfaces were parts of conic sections. Such aspheric figuring was, however, impracticable,[1] and Gregory suggested the use of a spherical reflecting mirror as well as the use of a small concave mirror to bring the image back to an eyepiece. This design was disapproved of by Newton, who however agreed that a form of reflecting telescope was the best way to tackle the problem of aberrations, having proved that the real trouble was chromatic aberration. In 1666 he built his first reflecting telescope, using a spherical primary mirror and a small *flat* mirror placed at an angle of 45° to direct the rays to the eyepiece at the side of the tube. In 1672 Cassegrain, a Frenchman, suggested a third design of reflecting telescope, in which the small concave mirror of Gregory's design was replaced by a convex one. This gave a very much longer effective focal length than Newton's design; but like Gregory's, it met with Newton's disapproval. The Newtonian design was a practical answer to the problem of aberrations, but did not come into wide use until the eighteenth century.

As we have said, the advent of the telescope brought forth greater accuracy of observation, and allowed objects in the heavens to be examined in detail. This power to examine the Sun, Moon and planets exerted a profound effect as soon as it came into use. Galileo found that the Moon presented a surface of which part was clearly mountainous, while other parts appeared as though covered by large seas. The Sun showed spots which passed across its surface. Jupiter presented a sensible disk and, more important, a number of attending satellites. The observations of the Moon indicated, then, a body akin to the Earth; the spots on the Sun showed

[1] It has become introduced into certain types of optical equipment only since 1948, and even now it is not used in complex and accurately-figured lenses.

that this body had 'blemishes', and so underwent change, while the satellites of Jupiter gave a 'living' example of a body moving through space with other bodies dancing attendance on it. All these facts hit body-blows against the arguments which had been advanced to prove that the Earth must be fixed, and that the heavenly bodies were essentially different in nature to things terrestrial. Prejudice there was against this evidence. Gradually, however, the wide use of the telescope in Western Europe caused the critics to realize that they were beating the air. Yet it is sad to recall that Galileo did not live to see the day when vindication came to the astronomer and his telescope. His observations of Saturn had early shown that the planet appeared to have two satellites, but later on he could discern only the disk of the planet itself. As we now know, this was due to the rings round Saturn, changes in relative position of the Earth and Saturn, and the very thin nature of the rings themselves. To Galileo, however, it seemed as though Nature herself mocked him. Actually the problem was solved fourteen years after Galileo's death by Christiaan Huygens (1629–1695). Using a refracting telescope optically superior to Galileo's, Huygens observed both the large satellite Titan and also an appendage. Observing the rotation of the planet itself, and noting the continuous nature of the appendage, he realized that he was looking at a phenomenon unique in the Solar System: a planet with a ring-system.

Observationally Huygens provided three other important practical contributions. First, he developed a two-lens eyepiece, still known by his name, and he was thus able to correct for some of the image defects which had blighted telescopic observing. Setond, he investigated the motion of the simple and compound pendulums, and produced a mathematical formula[1] relating the time of oscillation with the

[1] The well-known $t = 2\pi \sqrt{\frac{l}{g}}$, where t = time of oscillation, l = length of the pendulum, and g = acceleration due to gravity.

THE NEW APPROACH: II. OBSERVATION 129

length. Moreover, he appreciated that the period of oscillation of a pendulum varied slightly with the terrestrial latitude at which it was used, a factor which later assumed importance. Third, he developed a practical pendulum clock, using a train of gears and driven by a descending weight. The latter invention was of considerable significance in astronomy, for accurate timekeeping is one of the essences of positional observations. His successful development of the pendulum clock much affected timekeeping, reducing the error in the clocks then available by about 50 per cent.

The seventeenth century also saw the establishment of the national observatory. The maritime power of England and France made clear to both nations the need for establishing a practical and effective method for determining longitude at sea. Indeed the need was such that it was appreciated that no time should be lost in taking steps whereby this might be done. The pendulum clocks of Huygens could not be used at sea, and there was no other form of timepiece giving anywhere near the accuracy required. The only apparently practicable solution seemed to lie in observations of the Sun, the Moon and, perhaps, the brighter planets and stars, made on board ship and checked against accurate tables of their expected positions. Unfortunately no tables of sufficient accuracy, at least for use with telescopic sights, existed. It was, then, clear that more and accurate observations of the positions of the heavenly bodies were required. In Paris, Louis XIV decided to establish an observatory, and invited Gian Domenico Cassini (1625–1712) to direct the institution. Cassini had been appointed professor of astronomy at Bologna at the age of twenty-five, a great honour for so young a man, and while there had enhanced an already sound reputation. Under his direction the new observatory obtained instruments from Campani and Divini, well-known Italian instrument-makers, and Cassini obtained the services of Olaus Römer from Denmark, and Christiaan Huygens from

Holland, together with the Frenchman Jean Picard (1620–1682). Cassini also recruited G. Richer (? – 1696), who made observations abroad of the meridian altitude of the Sun and the position of Mars, while Cassini and his colleagues made measures at Paris. Picard determined the length of a meridian arc with an accuracy superior to any previous measurement, and this was used by Newton in his gravitational studies. The simultaneous measurements in Paris and Cayenne led to a determination of the distance Earth to Sun more accurate than any previously made, and the value of 87 million miles was obtained. This was, of course, of the correct 'order of magnitude', and was a great step forward from the Greek determinations. Cassini lived long, and was followed as director of the observatory by his son, Giacomo, who was in turn succeeded by his son, Cesare Francesco, after which the 'rule of the Cassinis' came to an end.

In England, on 22nd June 1675, Charles II issued a Royal Warrant for the building of 'a small observatory' at Greenwich 'in order to the finding out of the longitude of places for perfecting navigation and astronomy'. The first astronomical 'observator' was John Flamsteed (1646–1719), who received the title of Astronomer Royal, and the observatory was designed, appropriately enough, by Wren, who was both an astronomer and an architect. Flamsteed had to supply his own instruments, as well as a skilled assistant, and his small and inadequate salary had to be supplemented by taking private pupils in astronomy and navigation. In 1684 his position improved, for he obtained the living of the parish of Burstow. He worked for thirteen years unaided, using a sextant of 7-foot radius, as well as other instruments, including a pendulum clock, which he provided himself. He made 20,000 observations of stellar positions. On the death of his father in 1688 Flamsteed became considerably better off financially, and employed his first assistant, Abraham Sharp, who was an excellent instrument-maker. Whereas the sextant had enabled him only to measure the distances between one star and another, without reference to any fundamental reference-point, Flamsteed was now able to afford a large mural arc which Sharp made for him. Observations could then be made of meridian transits of stars, and work commenced in 1689. Flamsteed's observations were of exceedingly high precision, and superior to any made either before, or during, his time. The tradition of positional observations of exceedingly high accuracy which he established has been maintained at the Royal Greenwich Observatory ever since. In 1670 Flamsteed published an almanac, but otherwise no observational results were forthcoming. Flamsteed wished to reserve publication until his observational programme had been completed; and because he had provided his own observing equipment out of his own funds, he looked on the matter as one of his own concern alone. Others, however, wished to make use of the results, and moreover the observatory had been founded with the express purpose of assisting navigators, who were still being left with tables far less accurate than they need have been. Finally Flamsteed was forced to deposit his observations under seal with the Royal Society, a committee of which was appointed as a 'Board of Visitors'.[1] An incomplete edition of his observations was published in 1712 under the title *Historia Cœlestis Britannica*, much to Flamsteed's resentment. Later, under a new political administration, Flamsteed was able to obtain the majority of the printed copies, and these he burned publicly. He then untertook the provision of a revised edition. Although he died in 1719, his assistants Sharp and Crosthwait saw the volumes through the press, and the work was published in 1725 as the *Historia Cœlestis*. It was a monumental work, containing a catalogue of 3,000 stars with positional errors not greater than 10″, and represents the results of 44 years of painstaking observation.

[1] The Board still continues, and a Royal Warrant for its appointment is issued as each new sovereign ascends the throne.

In 1720 Flamsteed was succeeded as Astronomer Royal by Edmond Halley. Before his appointment Halley had already done much to further astronomy. His work in the dynamical field has already been mentioned, but observationally he had supplemented the work of Hevelius and Flamsteed in the northern hemisphere by cataloguing 360 stars visible only in the southern hemisphere; he had observed the motion of the Moon, and he had published observational papers on a star-cluster in Hercules, on meteors, and on nebulæ. Moreover he had, in 1710, prepared an edition of Ptolemy's star catalogue and, by comparing observations made in his own day, he was led to conclude that the stars themselves were not fixed in space, but had their own 'proper motions'. His paper putting forward this important idea was published in 1718. As Astronomer Royal, Halley was financially in a better position than Flamsteed. He had not only his stipend as Astronomer Royal, but also that of the Savilian Professor of Astronomy at Oxford, a position which he still continued to hold. However, even these two salaries were insufficient. Flamsteed's widow had claimed her husband's instruments from the observatory, and Halley, with his customary tact and diplomacy, had managed to extract £500 from the Board of Ordnance; and at a royal visit to the observatory in 1729 he managed to have his salary supplemented by half-pay of a Post-Captain.[1] He forthwith equipped the observatory with a transit instrument, and in 1724 an 8-foot quadrant made by Graham, a leading instrument-maker of the day and inventor of the 'dead-beat' escapement for clocks, by means of which their accuracy had been much increased.[2]

---

[1] Between 1698 and 1700 Halley had been commissioned by the Admiralty to chart magnetic variation, and had voyaged over the Atlantic, while in 1701 he charted the English Channel. A *Post-Captain* is one who has had command of a ship for not less than three years and Halley was, therefore, qualified.

[2] Huygens' development of the geared pendulum clock had reduced the mean errors of clocks by a considerable margin, Graham's dead-

The tradition of careful telescopic observation was established, and the re-determination of fundamental information such as the positions of the planets, and especially of the stars and the Moon, provided material for consideration by the theoretical astronomer. At the same time the telescope was being used for penetrating further into space, and it was found that as telescopic power was increased, more and more stars could be observed. In the year of his accession to the directorship of the Royal Observatory, Halley published an important cosmological paper in which he advocated the infinite extent of the universe and showed the fallacy of the argument, previously current, that if this were so then the sky should be bright at night. Halley supported the idea of an infinite universe. He countered the argument that, if the number of stars were infinite, then the sky should appear bright at night by claiming that, even if the stars were evenly distributed, the light from the more distant ones would diminish to a greater degree than their distances would increase. This he believed would be so 'even in the nicest Telescopes' and he quoted his observational results and those of others as evidence. His practical work at the observatory was concerned primarily with the Moon. Flamsteed had produced an excellent star catalogue, but had made comparatively few lunar observations. Halley decided that the method of measuring the apparent distance of the Moon from catalogued stars would be the best method, or at least the most practicable one, of determining longitude at sea; and he proposed to observe the Moon through a complete Saros – that is to say through one complete period of revolution of the nodes of its orbit, a period of 18 years. Considering that he was sixty-four years of age when he became Astronomer Royal, Halley was bold indeed to contemplate such a scheme. However, from

---

beat escapement had further improved matters, but final really accurate timekeeping arrived with Harrison's fourth marine chronometer which had the amazing accuracy of $\frac{1}{3}$ sec. per day.

1722 to 1739 he observed with such diligence that he never missed a meridian transit when one was visible. In 1731 he reported progress to the Royal Society, and showed that his observations would provide results giving the Moon's position correct to 2′, which meant an accuracy of position in longitude, at the equator, of 69 miles. He was urged, especially by Newton – who was President of the Society – to publish, but Halley resisted all pressure because he wished to prepare new lunar tables, and feared plagiarism. In the event the tables were not published until nine years after his death. The problem of longitude at sea was, however, solved in a practical way by John Harrison, who invented a temperature-compensated chronometer which was spring driven, with a balance-wheel instead of a pendulum for regulation, and which could successfully be used at sea.

Technical developments in observing equipment continued. Robert Hooke invented the very useful universal joint, which still goes under his name, and is of considerable use in providing control of the motion of a telescope from the eye-end. Hooke also made a micrometer which measured positions to an accuracy of 1″, and built an equatorial mounting with a clock[1] drive so that a telescope mounted thereon would automatically follow the stars, the mechanism taking account of the Earth's diurnal rotation. The helioscope was another of Hooke's inventions. It was an ingenious device for enabling observations of the Sun's disk to be made without danger to the observer. It consisted of an object-glass and two parallel plates of dark glass. The rays from the object-glass were reflected back and forth by the dark glass plates and finally, much reduced in intensity, were observed in an eyepiece.

A new step forward in the development of the telescope

[1] It must be remembered that a driving clock has, and needs, no escapement. This is because its purpose is to provide a continuous driving motion.

came in the eighteenth century from the work of Chester Moor Hall. Hall was concerned, as Newton and others had been, with the problem of chromatic aberration. He proposed the construction of an achromatic object-glass using two different kinds of glass, each having a different refractive index. According to Newton's ideas this proposal would not be effective, but Hall argued that as the eye was constructed so that the light passed through a lens and then through a liquid – the 'humour' of the eye – so then fully achromatic vision was the property of all eyes and, further, that because the lens and humour had different refractive indexes, a telescope objective constructed on the same principle must be successful. In 1757 John Dollond fabricated such a lens, and the achromatic refractor was born. However, it must be noted that Hall was wrong in his theory. We do not see chromatically aberrated images, it is true, but although the reasons are as yet not fully understood,[1] it is certain that the cause is not the different refractive properties of the lens and the humour. The wrong theory, but the right results! Dollond's achromatic objective was not all it might be; flint glass was difficult to make and even more difficult to prepare without bubbles and free from strain. Improvement came at the beginning of the nineteenth century when Guinaud, a Swiss optician, was successful in casting flint glass lenses, and in 1817 an achromatic refractor of the unprecedented aperture of $9\frac{1}{2}$ inches was installed by Fraunhofer at Dorpat. At the beginning of the nineteenth century, too, attention was also paid to the design of eyepieces and to the mounting of the instruments themselves. The refractor reached its peak of development in the last decade of the nineteenth century with the construction, in the United States, of giant instruments at Lick Observatory

[1] Recent (1959) investigations clearly indicate that the colour mechanism of the eye does not operate according to a three-colour stimulus as has been widely accepted since the time of Young (1773–1829) and Maxwell (1831–1879). How it *does* operate has still to be discovered.

in North California (36-inch aperture) and Yerkes Observatory, Chicago (40 inches). The reflecting telescope is, as we have already remarked, an instrument which is inherently free from chromatic aberration, and, moreover, it can be made with apertures considerably in excess of those possible with refractors. The reason is, of course, that in a reflector the glass for the mirror is only a 'vehicle' to support the reflecting surface, and the specification is therefore not so stringent. Moreover, the larger the diameter of a refractor, the thicker must be the lens components, and the more severe is the absorption which the light suffers; in addition, in the reflector there is only one surface to be figured, while in an achromatic object-glass there are four.

In the early stages of the development of the reflector, however, glass was not used as the reflecting surface. The material made use of was speculum metal, which was, in essence, an alloy of copper and tin, although minor changes in composition were made by various constructors. Newton used speculum metal, as did his contemporaries. The same material was used by William Herschel (1738–1822), and by the Earl of Rosse (1800–1867).

William Herschel was an amazing man. Born in Hanover, he became violinist and oboeist in the Hanoverian foot guards, in which his father and elder brother also served. However, he had always been interested in astronomy, and also much disliked his life in the foot guards. He voluntarily left the Hanoverian Army, and came to England; his formal discharge being obtained for him by his father in 1762. Herschel first worked as a music copyist in London, then as instructor to the band of the Durham Militia, and at the same time took in private pupils. He also composed many orchestral pieces, and took a wide interest in many subjects. Thus Herschel worked in various places up and down the country, finally settling down in Bath as organist of the new Octagon Chapel. His sister Caroline joined him in 1772, and his musical work continued. However, by 1773 Herschel was engaged in astronomical observation, and in attempting to build reflecting telescopes. He became an expert constructor of astronomical reflectors, but still continued his professional musical activities. In 1776 he set himself the task of making a reflector of 20-foot focal length, and he also developed his own version of the reflector, in which the primary mirror is placed at a small angle to the optical axis and viewing is carried out at the front edge of the tube, thus obviating the need for a secondary mirror or prism. Herschel continued his two lives, the astronomical and the musical.[1] Finally, after a brief sojourn at Greenwich and observations with Maskelyne, then Astronomer Royal, he established himself at Datchet, near Windsor, with a pension from the King so that he could devote his whole time to astronomy. A Royal pension was also paid to Caroline to act as his assistant. As a telescope-maker Herschel was unsurpassed. When his 20-foot instrument was temporarily set up at Greenwich it far exceeded in quality anything at the Royal Observatory. This telescope had only a north–south movement, and a speculum mirror $18\frac{3}{4}$ inches across. In 1789 Herschel designed and built a telescope of 40-foot focal length, but he carried out most of his observing with the 20-foot instrument. During his lifetime he built 430 parabolic mirrors, and carried out an astounding observational programme.

A large reflector was also used by William Lassell (1799–1880), but the greatest of all telescopes used in the nineteenth century was that of the Earl of Rosse, with a speculum mirror 72 inches across, and a focal length of 54 feet. This was built in 1845, and mounted in a north–south direction between two brick walls. With this immense machine Lord Rosse was

---

[1] In his diary for January 1782 Herschel recorded the following delightful statement: 'I gave up much time to astronomy and also attended many scholars. Some of them made me give them astronomical instead of musical lessons.'

able to see further into space than any man before him; but as might be expected, much that he observed was hardly believed, as no other astronomer could confirm or deny it. And there was no means of recording the observations made, except the personal one of preparing drawings.

From the fortuitous discovery of Lippershey in 1608 and the early instruments of Galileo, the telescope developed in less than 300 years into optical giants which could allow astronomers to see into space far beyond our own Galaxy, and observe comparatively near objects in detail to a degree which would no doubt have surprised the pioneers, imaginative though they were. Yet, besides the telescope, there were two further observational developments which took place in the nineteenth century. These opened up new possibilities, and gave rise to new studies and standards of precise measurement which, in a science so dependent upon precision, were bound to exert an effect which was nothing short of revolutionary. These developments were the advent of the spectroscope, and the invention of photography.

In his experiments concerning light, Newton had shown that white light could be spread into a coloured band or spectrum by passing it through a prism. In addition he found that if the light were passed through a second prism set in the opposite sense to the first, the colours were re-combined and appeared once again as white light. The dispersion of white light into colours could be continued, provided the source were bright enough, by using more than one prism, all the components being set in the same sense so that their dispersive powers reinforced each other. Newton and his contemporaries discussed at length the formation of colours, the nature of light and other related topics, and Newton's own views were published in his *Opticks*, the first edition of which appeared in 1704. But no one seemed to consider turning a prism to celestial objects other than the Sun, and still less of making a spectroscope. It was not until almost a hundred years later, in 1802, that William Hyde Wollaston (1766–1828) constructed a spectroscope in which the light entered through a narrow slit, passed to a prism, and was then examined. Using sunlight, as Newton had done, Wollaston found that the bright coloured spectrum was crossed by dark lines. The technique was applied by Joseph Fraunhofer (1787–1826), who saw that there were at least 1,000 lines, and who set himself the task of 'mapping' them. He mapped some hundreds, and on turning his telescope and spectroscope to the planets he found that the same lines were also present. However, when he applied his equipment to the stars themselves he again found that lines were visible, but that in this case the lines differed from those seen in the spectra of the Sun and planets. Fraunhofer was therefore firmly of the opinion that the dark lines which Wollaston had first seen, and which he himself had mapped, originated in the Sun itself. But how and why did they so originate?

For an explanation of the mechanism by which the lines are generated, we must turn to the laboratory chemist and physicist. As early as 1752 Melvil had discovered that flames tinged with metals or salts give spectra of bright lines against a dark background, and in 1823 Sir John Herschel (1792–1871) had suggested that the appearance or non-appearance of such lines might provide a test for the presence or absence of metals. Foucault (1819–1868) in 1849 examined the spectrum of the light which was generated between the carbon poles of a voltaic arc, and noticed how the two yellow lines which appeared coincided with two of the dark lines observed by Fraunhofer, and named by him 'D' lines. Foucault also found that if sunlight were passed through the arc, then these D lines appeared darker still, and he concluded that 'the arc presents us with a medium which emits the D rays on its own account, and which at the same time absorbs them when they come from another quarter'. The way was now becoming clear for a theoretical explanation of the 'Fraunhofer' or solar lines, especially when in 1855 the American physicist David Alter examined and described the spectra of hydrogen and other gases. In spite of the suggestion made in 1832 by Sir David Brewster (1781–1868) that, as some of the dark lines increased in intensity at sunset, they must be due to absorption in the Earth's atmosphere, the first attempt at a general theoretical explanation was given by Sir Gabriel Stokes (1819–1903). Stokes suggested that any mechanical system will absorb energy which falls on it with a rhythmic periodicity coinciding with its own natural period of vibration. He then applied his thesis to the Sun, and proposed that an outer envelope of gas absorbed the energy of those particular rays which had an oscillatory period equal to their own and emanated from a hotter interior. The light received by the spectroscope would then be deficient of certain frequencies or wavelengths, and black lines or gaps would result. A general theoretical hypothesis was put forward in 1859 by Gustav Robert Kirchhoff (1824–1887) and Robert von Bunsen (1811–1899) who, unaware of the work of Foucault, used incandescent lime as a source of a continuous spectrum and passed this light to a spectroscope, first through an alcohol flame into which they put common salt, and, in a second series of experiments, with lithium placed in the flame of a Bunsen burner. The first set of experiments produced dark D lines, the second a dark line which they could not discern in the solar spectrum they used. They concluded then that sodium was present in the Sun, but that lithium was either absent or at least present in quantities too small to be discernible.

Bunsen's and Kirchhoff's experiments disposed at one blow of the statement by Comte, referred to in the last chapter, that man would never know of what the stars were composed, and is a 'classical' example of the danger of firmly stating 'what one can never know'. Kirchhoff found that dark-line (absorption) spectra and bright-line (emission) spectra were the same so far as composition of the gases was concerned, and he proposed 'laws' for the formation of spectra based on the results of his work and that of Bunsen. The next step after this fundamental theoretical and experimental work had been done, was to apply the results to the study of the universe. Clearly this was a new and very promising line of attack, and, what is more, was made even more important in view of the proposals of Christian Doppler (1803–1853) that the colour of a light-source should be altered if that source were moving towards or away from the observer, i.e. moving in the line of sight. Doppler's principle[1] was based on an analogy with the alteration of pitch of the sound of a body moving in similar fashion, and its particular application to the spectrum was made by Fizeau (1819–1896) in 1848, a year after Doppler had announced his ideas. Fizeau pointed out that the effect should be discernible not as a colour change, but as a shift of the spectral lines. This was an important discovery, for it enabled line of sight velocities of celestial bodies to be obtained, and is even now the only method of making such determinations.

The beginning of systematic observational astronomical spectroscopy was due to Father Angelo Secchi (1818–1878). Secchi observed the spectra of many stars, and in 1867 put forward a classification, dividing spectra into those which showed mainly hydrogen lines, those where the lines of metals were the primary constituents, and those with bands due to molecular absorption. Secchi's work was developed by Sir Norman Lockyer (1836–1920). Lockyer tied up observed results with laboratory investigations, and put forward his *dissociation hypothesis*. This was an important proposal, in which it was suggested that the atoms of all elements were

---

[1] The shift is given by $\lambda' = \lambda\left(1 + \dfrac{v}{c}\right)$, where λ' is the new wavelength, λ the original wavelength, v the velocity of approach or recession and c the velocity of light.

groupings of similar basic constituents. Lockyer further realized that the excitation of atoms produced the results observed in spectra, and, most important of all, he appreciated that temperature was the most potent factor in causing excitation. A new classification was proposed by the American astronomer J. W. Draper (1811–1882) and this, modified in certain details, is still used. It is, in effect, a classification according to temperature. Another great spectroscopist was Sir William Huggins (1824–1910), who carried out much work on the position of spectral lines and observations of the 'Doppler'[1] shift, and in 1868 succeeded in making the first measures of the line of sight velocities of stars. The Doppler principle was also applied to the Sun in 1873 by H. C. Vogel (1841–1892). Vogel compared spectra of the approaching and receding limbs of the Sun and tied up the theoretical considerations with the Sun's rotational speed obtained from direct visual observation. 'Maps' of the solar spectrum were also prepared, and the identification of solar and terrestrial elements was begun. Many contributed to the work, which was extended beyond the visible spectrum. As far back as 1800 Sir William Herschel's son, Sir John Herschel, had demonstrated that heat rays were discernible beyond the visual red part of the spectrum, and soon afterwards Ritter (1776–1810) showed that there was an extension beyond the violet end. The identification of elements was the special province of Henry Augustus Rowland (1848–1901), who developed the grating spectroscope, in which instead of a prism there is used a glass 'grating' with lines of the order of 40,000 per inch, forming a spectrum by diffraction. Rowland's map gives some 16,000 solar lines. However, by 1878, due primarily to the work of Lockyer, the number of *elements* recognized was 33, the first (hydrogen) having been identified in 1862 by A. J. Ångström

[1] It would seem that, more correctly, this should be termed the *Fizeau Shift*. The term *Doppler Shift* is, however, always used.

(1814–1874). The most dramatic of all these identifications was made in 1895 by Sir William Ramsay (1852–1916), who found in the mineral cleavite an element which had been named 'helium' by Lockyer.

This brief sketch of the beginnings of astronomical spectroscopy will have to suffice to show what a great step forward was made by this new limb of observational technique. The theoretical implications of the new astrophysical research took time to develop. Meanwhile another new factor had entered the field of astronomical observation, a factor which was to assume great significance. The principle of photography can be traced back to the early part of the seventeenth century. In 1614 Angelo Sola had noticed that silver nitrate turned dark when exposed to sunlight, and over a century later, in 1727, Johann Schultze managed to record shadow images using a mixture of chalk, silver, and nitric acid. A few years after Schultze's experiment, Carl Scheele found that the blackening in sunlight of silver nitrate caused pure silver to be formed, and he also discovered that the violet end of the spectrum was more effective than the other visible rays. At the beginning of the nineteenth century Sir Humphry Davy (1778–1829) and Thomas Wedgwood described the production of shadow images using paper impregnated with silver nitrate, but no method was evolved of fixing these images so that they did not continue to blacken. However, in France, Nicephare Niepce (died 1833), using a coating of asphaltum, actually obtained a permanent image by exposing the asphaltum in a camera obscura and then dissolving the unexposed portions by using a solution of sweet oils. By inking up the remaining asphaltum, the picture could be printed on to paper. The sensitivity of the material was exceedingly slow and the process cumbersome. Niepce tried to improve it, and in 1829 he joined forces with a compatriot, Louis Jacques Mandé Daguerre (1789–1851). On Niepce's death Daguerre returned to experiments using silver salts as the light-sensitive material, and in 1839 developed the practical, and soon widespread, system known as the Daguerrotype. The method of preparing a Daguerrotype was to rub a copper plate with silver mixed with pumice powder and sweet oil, and then to wash the treated plate in distilled water and nitric acid. Finally, in a darkened room, the plate was exposed to iodine vapour, which then formed a light-sensitive layer of silver iodide. The completely sensitized plate was next exposed from 4 to 40 minutes, the time depending on the brightness of the image. A latent image was obtained, and this was made visible by exposing the plate, again in the dark, to mercury vapour. When the image was completely developed it was fixed by being washed in a hot solution of distilled water and common salt or hyposulphite of soda. The Daguerrotype came into comparatively wide use, and in 1845 Foucault and Fizeau used the method for obtaining a picture of the Sun. Five years later, G. P. Bond (1789–1859) successfully made a Daguerrotype of the Moon.

The next practical development was the calotype. William Henry Fox Talbot, an artist, was in the practice of using a camera lucida,[1] and after a number of experiments he managed to make a suitable light-sensitive paper along the lines of Davy's and Wedgwood's method. He soaked his paper in baths of common salt and silver nitrate. He made contact negatives of the shadows of various objects and then fixed his results either with common salt or potassium iodide, but this fixing was inadequate. Sir John Herschel became interested in Talbot's work, and coined the word 'photography' to describe the process. Moreover, when Talbot had produced prints on sensitized paper from an original fixed photograph, Herschel suggested the terms 'negative' and 'positive', which have since become so well known. Originally Talbot's material required about an hour's exposure, but by sensitizing the material a number of times and then exposing it when wet

[1] A type of camera obscura.

THE NEW APPROACH: II. OBSERVATION

he was able to reduce the period to about ten minutes. Talbot's first successful photograph (as against shadow-picture or 'photogram') was taken in 1835, and by 1839 he was using sodium thiosulphate (hypo), at Herschel's suggestion, for fixing his results, and the effect was permanent and unfadeable. Talbot improved the sensitivity of his material by soaking his paper in silver nitrate and gallic acid, and after a short exposure of the order of half a minute, he found that he could build up his image by further treatment in the same solution. However the use of paper as negative material limited, because of the texture of the paper itself, the fine detail which could be recorded.

The next step forward was the invention, by Frederick Scott Archer, of the wet collodion process. Collodion,[1] discovered in 1847 and used as a protection for wounds, was combined by Archer with potassium iodide and coated on to a glass plate. He next dipped this plate, in the dark, into a solution of silver nitrate. While wet the plate was placed in a light-tight holder and exposed, still wet, in a camera by drawing aside a sliding panel in the holder. Development took place in pyrogallic acid or ferrous sulphate, after which the sensitive emulsion was stripped from the glass plate, fixed in hypo and washed again. Later the emulsion was allowed to remain permanently on the glass plate. The method, cumbersome though it was, gave brilliant images and fine detail, and also permitted numbers of prints to be made. It thus combined the advantages of the Daguerrotype and the calotype. The astronomer Warren de la Rue (1815–1889) was the first to apply the wet collodion process to astronomy. In 1853 he photographed the Moon, and in 1857 constructed a special solar photographic telescope (a photoheliograph) at Kew; soon these instruments multiplied, and photographic records of the Sun and its spots came to be made as a regular observational routine.

[1] An alcohol-ether solution of cellulose nitrate.

The next and most far-reaching development of the photographic process was the invention of the dry plate. A fast dry collodion plate was made in 1855 by J. M. Taupendt, but the use of gelatin instead of collodion brought the most successful results. Richard Maddox carried out experiments using gelatin, publishing his results in 1871, and in 1878 Charles Bennett improved the process by using cadmium bromide and silver nitrate as sensitizing material; Bennett's material was sensitive enough to give really brief exposures. This amounted almost to a photographic revolution. Plates could be obtained pre-sensitized, exposed when required, and developed at leisure. The experimental work for new emulsions passed from the hands of lone experimenters to those who could now manufacture sensitized plates for general sale, and who, in a short time, established companies which grew in size as the general use and specialized applications of photography developed. Plates sensitized to various parts of the spectrum were developed, and made generally available.

Sir William Huggins was the first to use the dry plate for astronomical purposes. The advantage of photographic recording of spectra compared with visual observations is hard to overrate, especially in studies concerned with the radial or line of sight velocities of celestial objects. Photography made it possible not only to record spectra for subsequent measurement at leisure, but also to record on the same plate, at the same time, and through the same spectrograph, the comparison spectra which are so necessary for precise measurement. Moreover, in obtaining measures of positions of stars, the photograph is much superior to ordinary visual observation, however excellent the micrometer which is used. The reason for this is that once the star-field has been photographed, the plate can be inserted into a large, heavy, and accurately-machined measuring microscope, and measurements may then be made in a comfortable position, at leisure, and to an accuracy of fractions of a second of arc. Finally, photography provides a means of effectively increasing the aperture, and thus the 'space-penetrating power', of a telescope. This is, of course, due to the fact that a photographic plate builds up the image as the exposure continues, and so with a long exposure the sensitivity exceeds by far that of the human eye. So important were these factors that in 1886 Sir David Gill proposed the formation of an international organization for preparing a photographic atlas of the heavens. The scheme came to fruition, and the atlas contains the images of upwards of 100 million stars. Photography brought the truly achromatic reflector back into favour, and it would be no exaggeration to say that the advent of spectroscopy and photography virtually changed the face of observational astronomy, as well as certainly having a profound effect upon cosmological speculation.

Having taken a glimpse at these advances in observing technique, we must – before embarking on some remarks on twentieth-century cosmology – turn our attention to certain results which have since been further developed, and have provided cosmologists with a sound basis for their theories. A scale of space is obviously vital, and reference has already been made to the measures of the distance between the Earth and Sun (that is to say the astronomical unit a) made under the direction of G. D. Cassini at the Paris Observatory. Halley, in 1679, had used observations of the transit of Mercury for determining a, and he saw that the method was of practical application. Halley appreciated that a transit of Venus would give better results, because Venus is much closer to the Earth and therefore observations made from different terrestrial observatories would result in more easily measurable quantities. In 1691 he made more detailed proposals, and again in 1711 he published details of a 'method of durations' which he urged astronomers to use for the transits due to take place in 1761 and 1769. His suggestions were followed up by the French and others, and in 1824 were subjected to a careful examination by J. F. Encke (1791–1865) who derived from them the figure of 95¼ million miles as the value of a.[1] A value close to this had, as remarked in the previous chapter, been obtained from dynamical observations by Leverrier. Another attempt was made at using transits in the latter part of the nineteenth century. Transits of Mercury occurred in 1874 and in 1882, and photographic techniques were employed. A value of 92½ million miles was obtained. A few years earlier, in 1864, Struve and Foucault had used a method based on the velocity of light, details of which will be discussed presently. This method gave a value very close to that obtained by utilizing the transit of Mercury which has just been described, Struve and Foucault obtaining the value 94¼ million miles. The next attempt was made in 1887 by Sir David Gill, observing on Ascension Island. He observed Mars at morning and evening, working on a suggestion of Sir George Biddell Airy (1801–1892), the sixth Astronomer Royal. Gill obtained a value of just over 93 million miles, a value very close to that accepted today. All the nineteenth-century values showed an increase in accuracy over previous ones. The measures of the transit of Mercury, the work of Struve and Foucault, and of Sir David Gill agreed to within $\frac{12}{100}$ of a second of arc, and showed how precise astronomical measurement was becoming.

It was this increase in precision which allowed the annual parallax of some closer stars to be obtained, and brought about the first appreciation of stellar distances. James Bradley (1692–1762), who succeeded Halley as Astronomer Royal, made a valiant attempt to measure stellar parallax. He used the star γ Draconis, employing a telescope made by Samuel Molyneux (1689–1728) at Kew. In 1725 he noticed a shift of position, and continuing his observations in 1726, he noticed that the star moved back to its original position. Moreover, whereas a parallactic shift ought to have given a

[1] For fuller details of this method see Appendix IV.

THE NEW APPROACH: II. OBSERVATION

movement in the Sun's direction, the actual shift which he observed was perpendicular to this direction. He continued his observations, and discovered that the form of the shift depended upon the celestial latitude of the star under observation. Stars on the ecliptic moved in a straight line, those at the pole of the ecliptic described circles, and the stars between the pole and the ecliptic described ellipses of varying eccentricities. The major axes of these ellipses were observed to lie in the direction of the Earth's orbit. After much consideration, Bradley at last hit upon the explanation. He realized that the observations provided definite proof of the Earth's orbital motion. The explanation which Bradley hit upon is known as the *aberration of light*, because this phenomenon of stellar displacement is due both to the small but finite time which light takes to travel through the tube of a telescope, and also to the fact that during this interval the Earth has travelled a certain distance in space due to its orbital motion round the Sun. The finite speed of light was, of course, known from the work of Römer in 1675, who had obtained a value for the velocity by observing eclipses of Jupiter's satellites. Not only did Bradley's work overtly demonstrate that the orbital motion of the Earth was a reality, it also, as mentioned in the last chapter, led to the discovery of nutation. Moreover, as he was able to measure parallax to an accuracy of $1''$, he was able to show that γ Draconis lay at a distance of not less than 400,000 times that of a.

The phenomenon of aberration can be used to determine the value of a, for the observations provide a relationship between the ratio of the orbital velocity of the Earth and the velocity of light on the one hand and the angle of displacement on the other. Foucault and Fizeau both made terrestrial measures of the velocity of light, Foucault in 1850 using a rotating mirror method and Fizeau, the year before, using a method utilizing a special toothed wheel. As already mentioned Foucault and Struve determined a by the aberration method. Thus Bradley's discovery was one of wide implications.

It will have been noticed earlier, no doubt, that when discussing spectroscopy, light was taken to be a wave disturbance. Newton had proposed what was primarily, although not entirely, a corpuscular or particle theory. Huygens and Hooke supported forms of the wave theory. In the nineteenth century the wave hypothesis became generally accepted, due to the work of Thomas Young (1773–1829) and Augustin Jean Fresnel (1788–1827), and the medium of transmission was held to be a weightless and non-resistive æther. Bradley had shown that the Earth's motion could be physically observed, and in 1887 Michelson and Morley set up an experiment to measure the speed of the Earth relative to the æther, thus providing experimental proof of the existence of the æther. On the hypothesis that the Earth did not disturb the æther (inherent in the proposal that the æther was non-resistive), then the æther and the Earth must be in relative motion. If then they measured the velocity of light in two mutually perpendicular directions, one of which lay aparallel to the direction of the Earth's orbital motion at the time of observation, a difference between the measures of the velocity c of light should be discernible. The experiment showed that no such difference existed. In consequence Michelson and Morley repeated their experiment six months later when, clearly, the Earth was moving in the opposite direction in space. Again the result showed no measurable difference. An attempt of a different kind was made in 1893 by Sir Oliver Lodge (1851–1940), who measured the velocity of light by using two heavy steel plates spinning at very high speed. He could, however, find no æther drag. The wave theory of light seemed to be in jeopardy, yet the preponderance of evidence supported it, and explanations were looked for elsewhere. These led to a revolution in cosmology and

THE NEW APPROACH: II. OBSERVATION

celestial dynamics in the early years of the twentieth century, and these will be referred to in the next chapter.

Cosmological developments in the twentieth century also arose from the increasingly precise observations which the nineteenth century provided. Bradley had tried unsuccessfully, as we have seen, to measure stellar parallax. The first successful measures had to wait until 1838, when three attempts were made, each yielding the long-awaited evidence. Friedrich Wilhelm Bessel (1784–1846) made his measurements at Königsberg. He selected a star with a very high measured proper motion. Since Halley's discovery of stellar proper motion, measures had been made, not least by Bessel himself, and because the star catalogued as 61 Cygni had a motion in excess of 5″ per annum, Bessel was of the opinion that this star was the most likely to yield a measurable result. Careful observations gave a parallax of 0·35″, a masterly observational result, and indicated a distance of six hundred thousand times that of the Earth to the Sun. Another measure of parallax, this time of the star α Centauri, was made in the same year at the Cape of Good Hope by the director of the observatory there, Thomas Henderson (1798–1844). Henderson obtained a value for the parallax of 1″, although subsequent determinations have given 0·75″. An attempt was also made by Friedrich Wilhelm Struve (1796–1864) at Dorpat, using a giant 15-inch refractor. Struve picked the very bright star α Lyræ (Vega) and obtained a value of 0·26″ for the parallax. The genuineness of this result as a true parallax observation is open to question, for more recent determinations have shown the value to be three times too large. However, be that as it may, later observers were stimulated to make further attacks on the problem, and by the end of the century the parallaxes of about a hundred stars had been determined. The advent of photography had not a little to do with this, and at present measures can be made if the parallax is not less than 0·003″.

A new development made during the eighteenth century, and more particularly during the nineteenth, was a more rigid approach to the question of determination of stellar magnitudes, and the application of this to studies of stellar distances. Sir William Herschel realized that if he used telescopes of different apertures, and that if, on observing two stars of different brightness, the dimmer appeared in the larger telescope to be equal in magnitude to the brighter when viewed in the smaller telescope, then, provided the ratio of the apertures of the telescopes was 1:2, this would also be the ratio of the apparent magnitudes of the stars concerned. Assuming all stars to be of equal intrinsic brightness, Herschel proposed the method as a means of determining stellar distances. This was in fact a method based on the inverse square law of the falling-off of brightness. He tried the method, and discovered the important fact of stellar variability which has since been followed up in greater observational detail. Herschel also discovered the existence of binary stars. Galileo had observed some double stars, but had suggested that they were merely due to an optical illusion, the two stars lying close to each other in the line of sight. By 1782 Herschel had catalogued 50 examples, and obtained evidence that each pair moved round its common centre of gravity. Thus he established the important principle that gravity operates at great distances, and presumably throughout the entire universe.

John Herschel used an artificial star as a standard for his own measures of stellar magnitudes. He measured 191 stars in the southern hemisphere, and expressed his results in terms of the brightness of α Centauri. John Herschel also noticed that a star of magnitude 1 was about 100 times brighter than one of magnitude 6. The next great step forward in precise photometry was made in 1850 by N. R. Pogson. He began by tying his standard to the great star catalogue of Bessel and Friedrich Argelander (1799–1875) known as the

THE NEW APPROACH: II. OBSERVATION 153

Bonner Dürchmusterung. Pogson standardized on the sixth magnitude, and then took the first magnitude as being exactly 100 times brighter than his standard. He then showed that, visually, brightness was discerned in such a way as may best be expressed as a geometrical progression.[1]

The telescope not only extended measures of precision in respect of stellar brightness and proper motions but stimulated other work. With Sir William Herschel's counting of stars in 3,400 selected fields, some idea was obtained of stellar distribution. Nevil Maskelyne (1732–1811), the fifth Astronomer Royal, and J. J. de Lalande (1732–1807) had measured the proper motions of fourteen stars by 1783, and this further stimulated Herschel to attempt an assessment of the motion of the Sun. The evidence of such few measures was not enough to give a truly statistical result, yet Herschel, perhaps fortuitously, was able to give a position to which the Sun appeared to be moving, and a velocity for this motion, which was confirmed about fifty years later by Argelander, who had 390 measures of proper motion to go on. He also suggested that the Sun lay at the centre of our own stellar system. Herschel obviously enjoyed using his telescopes, and made four complete surveys of the northern hemisphere stars. When he began these surveys, Nicolas Lacaille (1713–1763) and C. Messier (1730–1817) had catalogued about 100 hazy patches of light which had come to be called *nebulæ*. Herschel increased the number to 2,500, and for a time believed that all would be resolvable into collections of separate stars if only telescopic power could be increased. His son, John Herschel, extended his father's work by observing in the southern hemisphere, while the Earl of

---

[1] From Pogson we obtain the relationship of luminosities
$$\frac{L_1}{L_2} = \frac{L_2}{L_3} = \ldots = \frac{L_5}{L_6} = k \text{ and } \frac{L_1}{L_6} = k^5 \text{ whence } k = \sqrt[5]{100} = 2 \cdot 512$$
and hence $\frac{L_m}{L_n} = 2 \cdot 512^{(m-n)}$.

Rosse, with his giant reflector, noticed the spiral nature of certain nebulæ. These results were, in the next century, to be extended and be shown to have great cosmological significance.

Knowledge of the Solar System grew not only from Newton's gravitational considerations, but also due to observational work. The discovery of the rings of Saturn and its satellites, together with the four large satellites of Jupiter, have already been mentioned; by the end of the eighteenth century it had been found that Mars possessed two small satellites, and a fifth satellite of Jupiter had been discovered, while Saturn's total had been brought up to nine. But the most surprising of all the Solar System results were obtained by William Herschel in 1781, Giuseppe Piazzi (1746–1826) in 1801, and John Couch Adams (1819–1892) and U. J. Leverrier (1811–1872) in 1846. To Herschel fell the honour of discovering the planet Uranus, which is virtually only a telescopic object; he thus made the first discovery of a planet in recorded human history. Herschel also discovered that Uranus had two satellites. His discovery was followed up by William Lassell (1799–1880), who in 1851 discovered two further satellites. Piazzi's contribution was the discovery of a small planet with considerable orbital eccentricity lying between the orbits of Mars and Jupiter. Since Piazzi's discovery, the number of these small planets or *asteroids*, as William Herschel called them, has increased vastly, photographic techniques being first employed by Max Wolf at Heidelberg in 1891.

Detailed examination of the orbit of Uranus showed the existence of certain perturbations which could be due, if Newton's dynamics were correct, to a planet at a still greater distance from the Sun. The problem was of considerable complexity. It was however tackled in France by Leverrier and in England by Adams. Both obtained a solution, but actual observational confirmation was first made by J. G.

Galle (1812–1910) in Berlin. This was a great triumph for the concept of universal gravitation, and showed, too, the power which lay in Newton's bold hypothesis. A satellite to the planet was discovered by the indefatigable Lassell in 1846, the same year as the planet itself was first observed.

The Sun came in for its due share of observational study. Sunspots had been seen by Galileo, and Christopher Scheiner (1575–1650) had discovered certain bright streaks and patches called *faculæ*. Various hypotheses were put forward to account for them. It was suggested either that the spots and faculæ were volcanic in origin, or that the spots were high rocks in a luminous sea with the penumbræ as shores of sand. Alexander Wilson (1766–1813) carefully noted that the spots showed foreshortening when they reached the Sun's limb, and he suggested that the spots were cavities, postulating also that the interior of the Sun was dark and only the exterior was bright. Wilson's ideas were taken up by Sir William Herschel, who suggested that the Sun was in fact populated, protection being afforded by clouds from the hot luminous surface. Herschel and James Nasmyth observed the granular surface of the Sun, and an argument arose as to whether these granulations were evidence of primitive organisms. John Herschel noticed that the sunspots appeared in zones above and below the solar equator, never at the poles, and suggested that there was an atmosphere above the luminous surface of the *photosphere*.[1] The 11-year period of sunspot fluctuation was discovered by H. Schwabe (1789–1875) and further studies gave increasing information. The applications of spectroscopy from 1859 onwards changed the picture, and moreover showed how the prominences, first noticed in 1706 by Captain Stanyan in Berne, could be observed without a total solar eclipse. The physical nature of the Sun became appreciated and the idea that it supported life which had been advanced by Herschel could no longer be held.

[1] The name *photosphere* was used first by J. Schröter in 1837.

The last contribution which must be mentioned before we turn to the great cosmological developments of the twentieth century concerns comets and meteors. During the nineteenth century a number of bright comets visible to the unaided eye appeared, and, following the basic advances of Halley and Newton, orbital paths were computed. Comets with extreme eccentricity and short periods were discovered, and in 1846 a comet observed twenty years earlier by Biela appeared split into two parts. Further studies showed that the short-period comets appeared to be associated with the large planets Jupiter, Saturn and Uranus.

Interest was also taken in meteors. In the seventeenth century a fall of meteorites in France was frankly disbelieved, and it is reputed that the statements of eye-witnesses were altered so that the 'impossible' facts should not be further considered. However, in 1834 there was a fall near Paris. The veracity of the reports of this was proved by the well-known physicist Biot (1774–1864), who was commissioned by the French Academy of Sciences to look into the matter. From further observations it became clear that meteors had velocities approaching those of the planets in their orbits. In 1833 there was a great display of meteors, now known as the Leonids; this was correlated with a large shower which had appeared a year previously. Records were searched, and it was noticed that a rich shower had appeared in 1799. H. A. Newton of Yale predicted another maximum for 1866 and, with its appearance, the idea of orbital paths for meteors became confirmed. Also in the year 1866 a comet originally discovered in 1862 by W. Tempel (1821–1889) did not return, but in its place there appeared another great meteor shower. Leverrier and, independently, Giovanni Schiaparelli (1835–1910) calculated the orbit of this shower and found that it coincided with the orbit of Tempel's comet. Gradually, then, evidence became overwhelming that meteors and comets were closely related. This led Lockyer to propose a theory of celestial evolution in which all celestial bodies were formed from a condensation of meteoric material. The solid core of this work on meteors was, however, not only the appreciation of their connexion with comets but also the fact that systematization was brought into a subject in which, for centuries, the phenomena had been treated as sporadic and not amenable to any physical laws.

Since the seventeenth century and the invention of the telescope, progress in observational astronomy had been tremendous. In two and a half centuries, man's observational knowledge of the universe had increased in ways never dreamed of in antiquity, and the universe was found to be both vaster and more complex than ever previously believed. From the theoretical point of view, Newton's hypothesis of universal gravitation had been vindicated time and again, and had provided a firm setting against which the bright gems shown by the observers could be placed. The general picture formed was of a system of moving stars and gas, with the Sun a star and attended by planets, asteroids and comets. Nebulæ had been discovered, and the problem of their ultimate resolution into stars still awaited examination by larger telescopes. The shape of the general stellar system was thought to be a disk, and it was generally conceded that the correct large-scale picture had been formed and that only details needed 'filling in'. Such was the attitude with which astronomers entered the twentieth century. What has so far befallen the cosmological picture since 1900 we must now investigate. It is a surprising and, indeed, exciting story.

Chapter 8

THE TWENTIETH CENTURY

The observational programmes which have been sketched, continued unabated as the twentieth century came in. But then, of course, so they should – for our division into centuries is a purely arbitrary one. What, in fact, we find in the twentieth century is that the pace of astronomical investigation increased – as indeed it had been increasing ever since the seventeenth century – but at a greater rate. Investigations into the stellar universe by using photographic spectroscopy continued to bear fruit, and to give an increasingly broader picture of stellar motions. In 1868 Huggins had applied the Doppler principle to stellar velocities, and from 1887 onwards Vogel had applied photographic techniques. In 1889, a periodically variable spectrum had been found of a star in the constellation of Ursa Major, and after investigation it was found that the star was a binary system, so that here, by spectroscopic study, was a means of extending telescopic power. However, the problem of determining stellar distances still remained, for there was a limit to the smallness of the value of parallax which could be measured. The first crack at this nut was made by E. Hertzsprung (1873–), who in 1905 conceived of the idea of absolute magnitude. This was defined as the brightness which any particular star would have if situated at a distance from the Earth such that its parallax would be 0·1″. The concept provided a means of comparing intrinsic brilliancies,[1] and, as it turned out, had

[1] If L_M represents the absolute luminosity and L_m the apparent luminosity then $\dfrac{L_M}{L_m} = 2\cdot512^{(m - M)} = \dfrac{(0\cdot1)^2}{\pi^2}$.

wider implications. In 1905 the number of stellar distances known was still small, and Hertzsprung supposed, logically enough, that stars with large proper motions were likely to be the nearest. On this basis he derived a statistical formula from which he could compute a great number of stellar distances, and thus absolute magnitudes. He then found that stars of white colour seemed to be of similar luminosity, but those which were red were either intrinsically very bright or else very dim. He found, too, that there was a diminution in luminosity from white to red, with, of course, certain exceptions. This was correlated with the spectral classification of Draper which was mentioned in the last chapter. Similar studies were carried out independently by Henry Norris Russell (1877-1957), and their results showed that apart from the bright red stars, there was a relationship between a star's absolute magnitude and its spectral class. This immediately gave rise to a new method for determining stellar distances; for, assuming an inverse square law for brightness and distance (an assumption which is inherent in the absolute magnitude concept), then by observing the spectral class of a star its absolute magnitude could be obtained; other observations would give the apparent magnitude, and so the distance could be found. This was an important step forward for gaining a quantitative picture of the universe. Russell also put forward a new and revolutionary idea, based on these results.

It must be remembered that the scientific and, indeed, the religious world had been torn asunder after Charles Darwin (1809-1882) had, in 1858, published his *Origin of Species*. Darwin had proposed, with a wealth of observational evidence, a system of dynamic evolution. This had brought into one scheme the plethora of species with which the Earth is populated by proposing a continuous development from their origin to present-day status. The ramifications of Darwin's proposals had affected every field of human thought, just as Newton's idea of universal gravitation had, two hundred years before, left its effects in every field of human speculation. Examining the relationship between absolute magnitude and spectral class, Russell was moved to suggest a new concept – stellar evolution. He proposed that a star began its life as a bright red star, became blue-white, then white, and continued its career until it became red and dim. Perhaps this was more a stellar life-cycle hypothesis than a hypothesis of stellar evolution – unless, of course, one considers that different spectral classes are equivalent to different animal species. It is a question of the viewpoint which one takes. Be that as it may, Russell's conception bore fruit both for the study of stars themselves, and the mechanism by which they generate their light – as well as for the formation of cosmological conceptions.

Just as Darwin had suggested a mechanism by which his dynamic evolution operated, so Russell suggested a mechanism for stellar evolution. He supposed that a star began as a mass of diffuse gas, bright but at a low temperature. It then contracted; the temperature rose but because the surface area was less the brightness remained approximately the same. Contraction, he believed, would continue until the star could no longer be considered to behave as a 'perfect' gas, the contraction causing heat to be lost more rapidly so that the absolute magnitude became numerically greater (i.e. the intrinsic brightness fell). The new idea had a great vogue, but in 1924 Sir Arthur Eddington (1882–1944) found that Russell's conception could not account for the development of white dwarf stars, that is to say hot stars of white colour but low intrinsic luminosity. The 'perfect gas' behaviour was shown by Eddington to be applicable to all stars. Later research has shown that white dwarf stars far outnumber large bright red stars, and therefore that the absolute magnitude/ spectral class relationship should be regarded not as an evolutionary sequence but only as separate equilibrium states. In other words the relationship is static, not dynamic.

Stellar motions, first found by Halley, were tangential motions – or motions *across* the line of sight. Applications of the Doppler principle gave velocities *in* the line of sight, or 'radial' velocities. Under normal conditions these radial velocities could be found for all stars which yield a satisfactory spectrum, but tangential velocities need re-observation from year to year, and obviously take longer to collect, while the number of stars at any one time for which such determinations can be made is limited. J. C. Kapteyn (1851–1922) carried out statistical studies on tangential motions, and in 1904 announced that his evidence showed that there were two 'streams' of motion – a group of stars moving in one preferential direction, with a second group moving in another preferential direction, both directions being in an opposite sense. Kapteyn suggested that there appeared to be some evidence for a third group of stars which seemed to have no preferential direction at all. This work was carried forward by J. H. Oort (1900–) who performed a statistical analysis on radial velocities. Oort was able to carry out analysis with a considerable number of very widely-scattered 'samples', and in 1928 presented almost conclusive evidence for the rotation of our stellar system, thus correlating Kapteyn's three proper motion star-streams. Oort gave the centre of rotation as a point towards the densest parts of the Milky Way, namely in the Scorpio–Sagittarius area. He found the velocity of the Sun in this rotating mass to be some 200–300 km/sec., and its period of rotation as 250 million years. Previous starcounts had shown the feasibility of a disk-shaped system, and in 1920 Kapteyn himself had shown that if the system were in fact disk-shaped, then the Sun could certainly not be at the centre.

All this work required great telescopic power, and we must now refer to some of the large telescopes which came into being in the early twentieth century. As the century dawned, the largest reflector in existence was of 60 inches diameter, and in use by Dr A. A. Common in England. However, Common's telescope was not completely satisfactory, and a 36-inch reflector also used by him gave superior images. In the United States, Professor Ritchey in 1902 finished a 60-inch mirror for the Yerkes Observatory. A few years after its construction it was mounted on the summit of Mount Wilson in California, for by this time it had been realized that as clear an atmosphere as possible is required if full use is to be made of instruments of so large a size. Ritchey's 60-inch was a highly effective instrument; it had a silver on glass mirror, and because of the efficiency of its reflecting surface the light-grasp was greater than that of the Earl of Rosse's 72-inch speculum. Moreover, Ritchey used a truly effective equatorial mounting. Ritchey's example was followed by the construction of many other large instruments. The next great step came in 1916, when a disk of glass 100 inches in diameter, which had been cast in France before the first world war, was ground and polished by Ritchey. It was mounted at Mount Wilson, with all the engineering aplomb possible; and considering that the moving parts weighed 100 tons, its lack of tube flexure and its smooth movements showed an ingenuity of design and competence of construction which was really remarkable. The Mount Wilson Observatory was not only the possessor of the world's largest telescope, but could also boast of three special solar telescopes, two of which were mounted vertically. The image of the Sun was fed to all three by mirror systems, and this type of solar instrument allowed the use of heavy spectrographs with very wide dispersion. In 1918 a 72-inch telescope was mounted at Victoria, British Columbia, and was fitted with excellent spectroscopic attachments. The solar telescopes provided much raw observational material for the solar physicist, and in due course it became appreciated that the sunspots were cooler than the surrounding photosphere. John Evershed (1864–1956) discovered that there was a motion of vapours from the sunspots, and further knowledge was provided by the spectrohelioscope, invented by George Ellery Hale (1868–1938) and H. Deslandres (1853–1948). This instrument permitted views of the solar disk to be obtained in the light of any particular spectral colour, and by this means allowed of a visual penetration below the photosphere. Of course, solar studies were limited to what could be seen under normal conditions. The corona, for example, could not be studied except at the time of a total solar eclipse. But in the 1930's a new solar instrument was developed by Bernard Lyot (1897–1952). This was the coronagraph, a very ingenious device which at long last enabled the solar corona and its spectrum to be observed in full daylight, thus immediately providing solar physicists with a new and powerful means of investigation. The instrument also permitted 'slowed-down' (time-lapse) ciné films to be taken of the prominences, again without an eclipse, and these have provided useful evidence for study of the prominence movements, since the prominence motions can for the first time be seen as a continuous process. Lyot's equipment was designed to be used in thin atmosphere such as is to be found at altitudes greater than 6,500 feet. He himself used his coronagraph on the Pic du Midi in the Pyrenees, where as far back as 1881 an observatory had been founded at an altitude of more than 9,000 feet. Lyot's techniques have been applied by Waldmeier in Switzerland, by Menzel in Colorado, and also in Czechoslovakia and Italy.

The advent of large telescopes and the development of photographic techniques led to increasing accuracy of observations of position. For these to be fully effective, really accurate timekeeping was required. Developments of the pendulum clock which would, no doubt, have surprised Huygens had fortunately taken place, and just before the turn of the century Riefler had developed a temperature- and pressure-compensated pendulum clock, so arranged that the pendulum had but little work to do; its accuracy was quite exceptional. Riefler's approach of trying to arrange for the timekeeping pendulum to be free to oscillate without having to expend energy in order to actuate a clock mechanism was finally solved by Shortt, a civil engineer. Shortt hit upon the ingenious idea of using two pendulums. One, known as the 'slave', operated the clock itself, and at the same time did duty by activating the impulse drive to the 'free' pendulum; and according to the position of the free pendulum, the slave was itself regulated. In effect, then, the free pendulum acted as a regulator only, but with no physical work to do. The Shortt free pendulum clock is the acme of pendulum clocks, but more recent developments have turned to the harnessing of radio-frequency methods; these must now be described. Crystals of the mineral quartz, if cut in a particular way, have a natural frequency of physical vibration. This vibration can be set up by feeding the quartz with an alternating electrical current. When the frequency of alternation coincides with the natural frequency of the quartz crystal, the vibration of the crystal reaches a maximum. The basic principle of the Quartz Clock, then, is that a high-frequency amplifier feeds an alternating current into a crystal, and – and this is the point – the difference between the input frequency and the crystal's natural period is fed back to the amplifier, acting as a control to shift the input frequency until it reaches that of the crystal. Once equilibrium is reached the input frequency remains constant. The final result is that a crystal-controlled constant frequency is available for timekeeping purposes, and an accuracy of the order of one thousandth of a second per twenty-four hours can be obtained. For such accuracy the crystal itself must be kept at a constant temperature and pressure; in other words, under uniform physical conditions. It is possible that the quartz clock may be supplanted in pride of place by an 'atomic' clock. This is similar in principle to the quartz clock, for its operation also is based on electronic feed-back methods. The vibration regulator used is composed of ammonia gas, and the accuracy so far obtained is better than one part in a hundred million. This seeking after ever-increasing accuracy in timekeeping is, of course, important. The astronomer is responsible for providing time determination. At the present day, the need to provide accurate frequencies for alternating current supplies, and for broadcasting and telecommunications, means that the requirements of accuracy have increased. Moreover, such accuracy enables matters of a fundamental scientific nature to be brought to light, of which inequalities in the rate of the Earth's rotation are an example. The increase of accuracy is well shown up in observations made in 1901 of the close approach to the Earth of the tiny minor planet Eros. These observations were examined by Hinks who, in 1910, was able to announce a new and more accurate value for the astronomical unit a. An even closer approach of Eros occurred in 1931 and, by international agreement, widespread photographic observations were made. The laborious correlation and reduction of the results were made by Sir Harold Spencer Jones who obtained a value of 8·79 for the solar parallax – indicating a distance of 93 million miles for the Sun's mean distance. This last determination is of outstanding accuracy, giving the Sun's position with an error less than 0·002″.

The increases in telescopic power allowed of great space penetration. The problem of the nebulæ was attacked, and it was found that the spiral nebulæ, to which attention was first drawn by the Earl of Rosse, were definitely systems of stars and gas external to our own Galaxy, and at great distances from it. Moreover, these investigations showed that the spiral shape was not universal, but that 'barred' spirals and other more amorphous forms also existed. Nevertheless, the fact of the external nature of these galaxies was established, and quite clearly affected the general cosmological picture, especially in view of theoretical considerations which will be described below. But it was not only the evidence of the existence of extragalactic systems which came with the large reflectors. There were the additional, and cosmologically important, factors of the apparent recession of the galaxies, and the knowledge obtained of their distances.

The apparent recession was ascertained from the Doppler shift of the spectral lines of each galaxy. The question of the distances of these objects was, however, a problem. No assessment using the diameter of the Earth's orbit as a baseline could yield any result; after all, this method was useless for any but the nearer stars in our own Galaxy. It would also seem that distances obtainable using the spectra and absolute magnitudes would again fail to produce results. However in 1912 Miss H. S. Leavitt (1869–1921), working at Harvard Observatory, discovered a relationship between the fluctuation period of variable stars with short periods – the so-called Cepheid variables – and their intrinsic brightness. Cepheid variables have periods of variation of a regular kind but the important factor, which Miss Leavitt discovered, is that the actual period is directly proportional to the absolute magnitude. Harlow Shapley (1885–) next tackled the difficult task of correlating a particular period with a given point on the absolute magnitude scale. His work enabled him to fix the distances of many globular clusters and, from magnitude measures on these clusters, to discover the distances of others.

Unfortunately determinations of this kind are also liable to another possible source of error. In order to make an estimate of distances it is necessary, as we have said, to observe the apparent magnitude of Cepheids in the galaxy. This, in turn, requires an assumption of a law of diminution of brightness with distance. Terrestrially such a law is well known; illumination falls off inversely as the square of the distance of the radiating source. It was, therefore, a natural extrapolation to apply this terrestrial law to the apparent magnitudes of Cepheids. However, the assumption was made by astronomers 'with their eyes wide open', for R. Trumpler at Lick Observatory had carried out a comparison on the absolute magnitudes of stars in open clusters such as the Pleiades, and had concluded that within the conglomeration of stars, gas and dust which form the 'island' of which the Sun is a member, there in fact occurs an absorption of light on its way to the Earth.[1] Some correction for this absorption could be made and an inverse square law of brightness still used as a basis for measurement provided, of course, it was also realized that the amount of absorption was different at various wavelengths.

By 1913, then, the picture of the physical universe was that the Sun, its planetary system and all stars observable as separate points of light were part and parcel of an island system or *Galaxy* in space. Outside this Galaxy it was found that there were hosts of other galaxies, and with this the nineteenth-century question of the 'spiral nebulæ' and where they were situated had to a great extent been solved. Some true 'nebulæ' or clouds of gas were found to exist in our own Galaxy, and similar objects were seen to exist in other galaxies. Thus the picture of the universe became one of increasing vastness. Virtually all of the galaxies showed a shift of their spectral lines towards the red end of the spectrum – the well-known *red-shift* – and indicated that the objects outside our own Galaxy appeared to be receeding from us.

The discovery of interstellar absorption and the existence of external galactic systems had also laid a ghost which had originally received an attempted exorcism by Halley but which had been conjured up again by H. Olbers (1758–1840). Olbers had, in 1826, questioned the idea, prevalent in his

[1] This absorption was found to be of the order of 0·7 magnitude per thousand parsecs, that is to say per 3260 light years. The parsec is adopted as the unit because astronomers measure distances in terms of parallax and a parsec is that distance at which a star would have a parallax of 1", i.e. 3·26 light years.

day, that the universe was infinite in extent. He suggested that if it were, and if the infinite number of stars were all of similar brightness to the Sun (a not unwarrantable assumption), then the sky should be infinitely bright or, at least, have a brightness equal to that of daylight. The distribution of stars and interstellar gas into discrete centres (galaxies), together with the evidence for interstellar absorption, clearly disproved the validity of the suggestion. The resuscitated ghost was 'laid' by Carl Charlier during the 1920's, when he also suggested that the galaxies were not uniformly distributed.

Reference was made in the last chapter to the 'unsuccessful' experiment by Michelson and Morley, who tried in vain to measure the motion of the æther. Michelson and Morley had not obtained the result they sought and, indeed, expected. Nevertheless, it would be unwise to term their experiment a 'failure', for, clearly, it called for some explanation and this could lead to new knowledge. Various suggestions were proposed. In 1908 W. Ritz (1878–1909) realized that the results could be explained if it were assumed that the velocity of light depended on the velocity of the source emitting it. This explanation did not, however, square with other facts, not least the observational results of W. de Sitter (1872–1935), made in 1913, which showed that the motion of the components of a double star system had no effect on the velocity of light. Just before the turn of the century, G. F. Fitzgerald (1851–1901) had put forward the suggestion that, in view of the atomic nature of matter, a body moving with respect to the æther contracted by an amount depending on the velocity of the body. Unfortunately, like Newton's first law of motion, Fitzgerald's hypothesis could not be empirically tested. Fitzgerald's work stimulated H. A. Lorentz (1853–1928) to extend the hypothesis and produce equations expressing alterations in mass and time measurements for moving bodies. All these changes are of course significant only when the velocity of a moving body is very large, that is to say not infinitesimally small compared with the velocity of light itself.

By 1905 Albert Einstein (1897–1955) realized that the Lorentz equations in respect of length, mass and time – the Lorentz transformations – which made sense of other attempts, such as those of Sir Oliver Lodge, to measure the æther, were of great significance; and that it was a necessary corollary that all electro-magnetic phenomena, as well as the laws of mechanics, must be the same for all systems which were in uniform relative motion. Thus Einstein appreciated that measures, however precisely made, would, if undertaken on the Earth, have a certain value for phenomena at rest with respect to the observer and a different value for phenomena observed and measured from the Earth but taking place on a body moving uniformly with respect to the observer. Moreover, he saw that the converse would also be true. An observer on a body moving uniformly relative to us would obtain different values to those we ourselves would obtain, for phenomena which he observed occurring on the Earth. Such a concept was revolutionary, for it meant that the generally accepted ideas of time and space could no longer be held. After all, it is clear from the normal ideas we all have of time and the space in which phenomena occur that, if a stationary observer measures the velocity of light as, say, c, then an observer moving with uniform motion relative to him should obtain a different value.[1] Again, Einstein's concept also meant that one could not consider *any* place as truly fixed in space. All observational results must, therefore, be referred to some frame of reference; and all measurements made must, then, be relative to such a frame.

Newton's ideas had implicitly contained the idea of an 'absolute' or fundamental and basic space and time to which events could always be referred. In Einstein's view, no such absolute 'framework' existed, and it was clear to those who

[1] His value should be $c+$ or $c-$ the velocity of the moving observer.

could see it that a revolution in our thinking must take place. An additional and useful idea was put forward in 1908 by H. Minkowski (1864–1909). He discovered, on a careful examination of Lorentz's work, that a universal value for measurements made by any observer moving with uniform motion relative to a fixed frame of reference could be obtained provided the space and time measurements were both used and combined in a particular way. In other words, the original and widely accepted ideas of time alone and three-dimensional space alone, as descriptive backgrounds for phenomena, had now to be replaced by a broader conception involving both space and time in order that events might be given a universality of application.

These new approaches also brought about an emancipation from the Greek ideas of geometry which had been generally accepted as fundamental and as applying to the cosmos as a whole. There had, of course, always been a problem concerning Euclid's postulate on parallel lines. It will be remembered that according to Euclid, if we are given a straight line crossed obliquely by another, then through a point on the intersecting line, one line, and one line only, can be drawn parallel to the given line. This seems self-evident, but the intriguing fact is that no general proof of this has been discovered. The challenge of finding a proof was often taken up, and as often thrown down. However, the assumptions which form the basis of Euclidean geometry began to be examined critically in the nineteenth century. Gauss and F. Bolyai (1775–1856) discussed the subject at the beginning of the nineteenth century, while in 1826 Lobatchewski (1793–1856) proposed a self-consistent geometry omitting the parallel line postulate. Similar views were expressed a few years later by F. Bolyai, jnr (1802–1860). The next step forward, postulating an infinite number of parallels in place of Euclid's solitary line, was provided in 1854 by Riemann (1826–1866). Riemann's geometry is reducible to Euclidean when very

THE TWENTIETH CENTURY

small volumes of space are considered. Mathematical methods of handling the new concepts were developed, especially by Levi-Civita (1873–1941) in the first decade of the present century. These proposals of the mathematicians had generally been looked upon, if looked upon at all by astronomers, as interesting excursions with no real counterpart in the physical universe of stars and galaxies. The reality of a non-Euclidean geometry seemed to be on a par with the physical existence of the crystal spheres of earlier times. Yet when Einstein began his work on relativity, and Minkowski proposed his space-time concept, the work of Riemann and others assumed more practical significance. Einstein found that in order to develop a more general theory of relativity in which accelerated as well as uniform relative motions were considered, he had to make use of a concept of space less restricted than that of Euclid. In the event, Einstein's ideas developed along the lines which Riemann had formulated, and he proposed a geometry of space-time such that every region was influenced by the bodies occupying it. Moreover, Einstein identified the shortest distances between points in the new geometry (i.e. the equivalents of straight lines in the geometrical scheme of Euclid) with the motions of bodies in a gravitational field.

The development of a general theory of relativity and its corresponding geometry led to three conclusions which could be observationally tested. The first of these concerned planetary orbits. Newton's gravitational theory, using Euclidean space, had shown that the orbital path of a planet must be expected to take the form of a stationary ellipse. Einstein's proposals, however, led to a path which is virtually elliptical, but in which the ellipse itself must be considered as rotating about the centre of gravity of the sun-planet system. The rate of rotation depends on the eccentricity of the orbit. Mercury had the largest value of eccentricity of the planets then known (Pluto was not observationally discovered until 1930) and Leverrier, many years before, had claimed to have found a small motion[1] of the perihelion of the planet's orbit. Leverrier had suggested the existence of another planet closer to the Sun in order to account for the perihelion motion on Newtonian principles. Einstein calculated what, according to relativistic laws, the motion of the perihelion should be. His result tallied almost exactly with the value found observationally, and which had never hitherto been satisfactorily explained.[2] Other observational tests of Einstein's theory were sought. In addition to the movement of the perihelion of Mercury, it was appreciated that two other tests presented themselves. The second concerned spectroscopic observations. Because of the interdependence of space-time and the presence of matter, Einstein claimed that in a strong gravitational field, for example that of a star, the behaviour of atoms should be slowed down compared to the behaviour of similar atoms on the Earth. The companion star to Sirius is extraordinarily dense, and by 1924 observations of the star made by W. S. Adams (1876–1956) at Mount Wilson observatory confirmed Einstein's prediction. The third test concerned the behaviour of light in passing near a strong gravitational field. One of the findings of relativity is that as the energy of a body increases, its mass increases also. There was, in fact, found to be an intimate association between mass and energy, two concepts hitherto considered in separation. By the last decade of the nineteenth century the work of Clerk Maxwell (1831–1879) and Heinrich Hertz (1857–1894) had made it clear that light and other radiations were essentially electromagnetic in character, while it had also been conclusively shown by Maxwell that light exerts a pressure, and in certain cases this has since been verified experimentally. Thus light was not only a form of electro-

---

[1] The motion amounted to 0·43″ per annum.
[2] Einstein obtained a value of 0·42″ per annum but, because of the errors inherent in the observations, some consider the validity of this 'proof' as open to doubt.

magnetic energy, as was radiation of other frequencies, but also it appeared to possess the property of mass. Hence, with the inter-relationship of mass and energy postulated by relativity, Einstein was able to suggest that rays of light in passing near a body with a strong gravitational field would suffer deflection, and he calculated that for rays passing very close to the Sun such a deflexion should amount to more than $1\frac{1}{2}''$. This, the third observational confirmation was successfully made by Sir Arthur Eddington (1882–1944) and others in 1919 on expeditions to observe the total solar eclipse of that year.

The theory of relativity stimulated much work on the universe as a whole, and ushered in a new phase in astronomical investigation – the mathematical-physical approach to cosmology. With mathematical tools far advanced from those available to the Greeks, with a wealth of observational material provided by the telescope and its adjuncts of photography and spectroscopy, astronomers in the twentieth century have been able to construct 'models' of the universe which are broader in scope and more exciting in conception than any previous views. Einstein himself proposed a model in which the universe was not infinite in extent but which, at the same time, had a finite boundary. This necessitated a non-Euclidean space, and Einstein slightly adapted a metric of the type proposed by Reimann. In order that his general theory of relativity should be the basis of his model, he had to modify a little his gravitational law. This he did by introducing a new constant (the cosmological constant) which assumes significance only when the universe is considered as a whole. The extent (or perhaps it is less confusing to say the 'quantity') of space is dependent upon the quantity of matter in it. Although the principle of relativity did away with the concepts of absolute space and time, and married space and time together in a particular way, in his model of the cosmos as a whole Einstein returned to the absolute form. In other words, relativity space-time was used for discrete observers and their measurements, but a fundamental and separate space and time were made use of for the complete universe. There would seem to be a parallel here in outlook with certain conceptions once held concerning planetary motions. A great step forward – yet still, at the same time, a clinging on to certain ideas previously generally held and, apparently, self-evident.

Einstein's universe was static but unstable. If matter were subject to the slightest disturbance then the whole cosmos should expand or contract. Moreover, a slight departure from homogeneity would cause, with the passage of time, an increasing change to take place in the universe. It came then to be suggested that Einstein's model represented the universe as it was near the beginning of its creation. However, the relativistic laws could be satisfied by other models. W. de Sitter developed a different model which had a space-time construction that was independent of the matter within it. Any material masses introduced into the de Sitter cosmos would develop a continually increasing velocity and recede from any observer at whatever point he was situated. De Sitter did not use an absolute time concept, and in his model any observer's limiting horizon is where time appears to stop. This standing still of time is, of course, only apparent, and the horizon is different for each observer. The apparent decrease of the rate of passage of time with distance would give rise to a red-shift in the spectra of distant objects, and the shift would increase with increasing distance. The amount of such a red-shift could not, however, act as a replacement for the red-shift due to physical recession, but was supplementary to it. The de Sitter model has sometimes been termed an 'empty' universe, and it was suggested that while Einstein's model was that which would fit the cosmos in its infancy, de Sitter's gave a picture of the universe as it would become in its old age. De Sitter also made use of the cosmological constant, and as in Einstein's model, this constant took a positive value.

The next step, as might be expected, was to consider models in which the universe was no longer a static concept, but in which the curvature of space varied with time. The astronomical effects of such a model have been investigated by Lemaître and others. With a positive value of the cosmological constant and a truly expanding space, the observable material of the universe is continually decreasing as objects are accelerated beyond the limiting velocity, namely the velocity of light. It became clear, then, that there were a considerable number of possible models of the universe which could be formulated on the basis of the doctrines of relativity. All require a mathematical facility of a high order for their full understanding, and each contains factors which cannot readily be pictured because use has to be made of concepts which have no exact equivalence to terrestrial phenomena with which we are generally familiar. Nevertheless, while there may, from time to time, be a temptation to produce models which are mathematically elegant and yet have no certain parallel to the observational universe, it is generally true that the theoretical cosmologist has always been stimulated by the results of the observational astronomer, and has, as often, asked him for special observations in order to narrow the choice on this or that factor.

In the United States the large reflecting telescopes, especially the immense instrument in Mount Palomar with its 200-inch diameter primary mirror, have brought much grist to the cosmologists' mills. Particularly has the work of E. P. Hubble (1889–1953), M. Humason and Slipher aided the formulation of cosmological problems. In 1916 Hubble began an intensive study of the most distant nebulæ and he established a scale of distances, using the 'Cepheid variable' as a standard brightness source for some nearer galaxies, and general magnitude methods for those further away. In 1929 using his own observations and those of Slipher he put forward his 'law' connecting the distance of these galaxies with their speeds of recession. With Humason he continued his work, observationally penetrating further into the depths of space, and found that his law appeared to remain valid. More recent measures have continued this 'space-penetration', and have shown that the apparent velocities of recession of the most distant galaxies for which observational evidence has so far been obtained, reach an appreciable fraction of the velocity of light. Observational evidence has been helped on the optical side by the development of the Schmidt telescope. In 1930 Bernard Schmidt (1879–1935) developed a telescope with short focal length and an extremely wide field of view. The Schmidt instrument makes use of a spherical mirror and a 'correcting plate'. Photographically the f/ratio[1] of the Schmidt is similar to that of a fast photographic lens, ratios of f/2·5 being not unusual compared to f/12 or thereabouts for a conventional optical telescope. Developments have also occurred in the understanding of the formation of a photographic image,[2] and this has led to the production of specially designed and effectively faster astronomical plates, which also have an inherently high resolving power. In 1941 D. Maksutov of Moscow developed a modified form of Schmidt telescope, and recent investigations with the 200-inch telescope and the 48-inch Schmidt at Mount Palomar have led

---

[1] The photographic speed of an optical instrument depends upon the square of the effective aperture and the focal length. The ratio [focal length ÷ aperture] is expressed as an f/number. Thus an instrument of f/4 is twice as fast (i.e. requires half the exposure) as one of f/5·6 and four times as fast as a f/8 instrument.

[2] The formation of a latent image on photographic material is a complex process. An advance in understanding came in 1938 when Professor N. F. Mott and Dr R. W. Gurney proposed a detailed theory of image formation. From this has resulted a fuller appreciation of the effect of low intensity illumination on sensitized material, and thus the avoidance of low intensity failure. Materials for specific operation under such conditions are now provided.

to new estimates for the distances of extragalactic nebulæ. Humason, Baade and Hubble confirmed the validity of the absolute magnitude/'Cepheid' period scale determination of Shapley for the variables in the globular clusters, but found an alteration to be required for types of 'Cepheids' found in the galaxies; this alteration has increased the distances estimated for all galaxies by a factor of two. More recently Sandage and others have obtained results indicating that even a factor of two is insufficient. As we should expect, these new instruments and the techniques of using them which have developed, have broadened the observational picture.

We must now turn again to the theoretical cosmologist to whom they are the raw material for his hypotheses. Eddington constructed a model universe in which he tried to synthesize the observational evidence and the basic laws of physics. He took into account the relativistic laws of dynamics and the laws of behaviour of atomic and sub-atomic material as developed in the Quantum Theory. The Quantum Theory itself has, of course, had a profound effect on our understanding of the mechanism of radiation and the formation of spectra, and it will be recalled that its basis is the hypothesis that radiation is emitted in discrete and indivisible 'packets' or 'quanta'. Eddington had been struck by the work of P. A. M. Dirac (1902–), who in 1928 had shown that certain behaviour of electrons could be expressed in a mathematical form which had the same aspect whatever frame of reference were used. Moreover, Dirac's results could not be obtained from the methods used in general relativity. Eddington, therefore, saw that this aspect of the microscopic universe of the atom must be correlated into any model on a macroscopic scale, for the mechanism of stellar behaviour is essentially due to the behaviour of fundamental atomic particles and their constituents. Eddington's model of the universe was coloured, then, by the concept of 'similar aspect under transformation' or what the mathematician refers to as invariance.[1] Indeed he developed mathematical techniques for the study of invariants, and believed that the universe itself could be understood on the basis of certain 'constants of nature' which were invariants on the cosmic scale. Eddington accepted a finite universe, as Einstein did, but for a different reason. Eddington was impressed with the discovery of the ratio between the electrical and gravitational forces which exist between two electrons. This ratio is a very large number[2] and Eddington believed that this ratio must have some *raison d'être*. He suggested that this might be connected with the number of particles in the whole cosmos. In other words, Eddington was seeking an underlying reason for the way things turn out. There is perhaps a similarity in outlook in this aspect of Eddington's work, a metaphysical approach, which is basically similar to that of Kepler who, believing in the harmony of the universe, sought a literally harmonious planetary system and also the Pythagorean approach in which the universe is primarily a number concept. Eddington developed his ideas, using the observable universe as a back-cloth for his work on fundamental relationships. In his book *Fundamental Theory*, published posthumously in 1946, he claimed to have proved that many of the basic physical laws were direct consequences of our understanding of the fundamental nature of the cosmos, and the basic forms we adopt for measurement. It must be admitted that Eddington's work is of such a kind as is difficult, even for the expert, to assess, but it is clear that his whole approach is one of determining the nature of the universe from certain basic premises. The rôle of observation is secondary.

Cosmological speculation along similar lines to those

---

[1] In relativity the velocity of light c is always the same, however an observer is moving with respect to the emitting source or, put another way, however the co-ordinates between one observer have to be transformed to express the frame of reference of another observer. This velocity c is, therefore, an *invariant*.

[2] Of the order of 3×10^{42}.

THE TWENTIETH CENTURY

adopted by Eddington, in that it is based on a choice of basic premises, was formulated by E. A. Milne (1896–1950). Milne laid emphasis on the measurement of time which, clearly, is a fundamental factor in all dynamical physical laws. He worked on the basis of a uniformly expanding universe and the idea that the appearance and history of the universe was the same for every observer situated on a 'constituent particle' (which may be identified as a galaxy). While Eddington had evolved a model based on spatial measurement, Milne was concerned with time measurement and the passage of light signals, and used a hyperbolic or Lobatchewskian geometry of space. Milne concluded that the laws of nature are dependent upon the distribution of matter. He also proposed that the ordinary time scale to which we are accustomed in physics, and which is based on the concept of a regularly rotating Earth, could not be taken as fundamental. For the basis of time measurement Milne proposed another time scale (τ-scale) which is connected logarithmically with the ordinary time scale (t-scale). As we make our measurements using the t-scale, and because his model of the universe is expanding, Milne claimed that the laws of nature would change with time – they were to be considered invariant only with respect to the fundamental τ-scale.

Milne's proposals have been felt by many to be rather of an esoteric kind and rather removed from reality. Nevertheless, Milne's work has proved stimulating, and has again emphasized the fact that, on the basis of general relativity, a number of possible models may be proposed. Observational confirmation or denial is difficult to obtain and McVittie suggested in 1939 that theoretical considerations were of primary importance, and claimed that a hyperbolic type of space was the most profitable approach. However, as we shall mention shortly, there is an indication that completely new techniques may help in allowing a selection to be made. Since the proposals of Einstein and

Eddington, de Sitter, Lemaître and Milne, a new approach has been made by Bondi and Gold followed up by Hoyle and has received much support from McCrea and Lyttleton. Bondi and Gold proposed the uniform distribution of matter as a basic principle so that, neglecting local irregularities of clustering, the universe may be looked on as always in a steady state. This steady state extends backwards and forwards infinitely in time. Now it has already been mentioned that the red-shift in the spectra of galaxies indicates a recession proportional to distance. Attempts to explain the entire red-shift by physical mechanisms other than actual recession have been made, but none appear to be satisfactory; all have had serious objections lodged against them. Taking the recession as read, and a steady state universe, it is necessary to postulate the formation of new galaxies. The proposers of this new cosmological view have therefore put forward the idea of the continuous creation of material particles. The metric of the universe is static; it is not taken as expanding. 'Expansion' has been relegated to a recessional motion of galaxies which will in due course become unobservable due to velocities which, relative to an observer, exceed the speed of light. New galaxies are then formed from the material being continuously created. The mathematical consequences of postulating continuous creation are important in considerations of the whole cosmos, but negligible in local areas, where the equations of gravitation reduce to those of Einstein. This brilliant and novel theory has met with much criticism, primarily from those whose bias is towards physical explanations. The idea that matter is being continuously created *de novo* but with no physical creation-mechanism postulated has caused severe attacks. One is reminded here of the attacks made nearly three hundred years ago on Newton's concept of universal gravitation because, after postulating the concept, he did not provide any satisfactory explanation of its working. One thing, however, is certain. Whatever may in the years to come be the fate of the steady state theory, whatever new hypotheses may be proposed, it has provided much stimulation, and has produced a 'new look' in cosmology with wide implications.

The twentieth-century attacks on the cosmos as a whole have led also, in conjunction with developments in theoretical studies on the nature of matter, to speculations on the formation of the Solar System and on the age and formation of the universe. These speculations have involved many factors, and have been assisted by work on the internal constitution of stars and the dynamics of binary systems and clusters. Sir James Jeans (1877–1946) examined mathematically the stability of rotating liquid masses, and showed that gravitational instability could lead to the formation of stars in the outer parts of a galaxy. He suggested that the Solar System was formed by the approach of a star to the Sun, whence the stream of gaseous matter produced would break up, those parts captured by the Sun forming planets. He took a long time scale for the age of the universe. He suggested it had been formed some 10^{12} years. Eddington, Chandrasekhar, Unsöld, Hoyle and Rosseland have worked on the problem of stellar constitution, and the generation of stellar energy has been considered especially by Eddington, Berthe, Weizsäcker and Gamow, Eddington as early as 1929 suggesting sub-atomic energy as the originating source. Coupled with further investigations and developments in the field of nuclear physics, the sub-atomic generation of stellar energy has now become universally accepted. This in turn has had an effect on ideas of the age of the universe. Further work on the dynamics of open clusters, of which the Hyades are an example, and more closely packed clusters like the Pleiades, have been now found to lead to an age of the order of 3×10^9 years. Jeans suggested that the kinetic energies of the stars were such that, assuming an originally random distribution, they showed characteristics of motion which must have taken at least 10^{11} or 10^{12} years to develop. However, more recent work has shown significant deviations in the kinetic energy of certain types of stars; and, moreover, the realization that our galaxy is in rotation has led to the rejection of Jeans' long time scale figure. Jeans' supposition on the formation of the Solar System has also been replaced. Hoyle and others have attacked the problem, and it has been suggested that the Sun was once a member of a binary system; considering the great number of binary systems which do, in fact, exist, this is a fair enough suggestion. It has, then, been postulated that the Sun's companion was drawn away by the collision of another star and that the Sun captured some of the gas resulting from the encounter. Alternatively it has been suggested that the companion star became a supernova, in which case the explosion of an envelope of hot gas would both have driven away the companion and left behind gas from which the planets could have been formed. With the probability that the major constituent of stars is hydrogen and the evidence now obtained on the sub-atomic transformation of elements, this theory not only provides the *modus operandi* of formation but also an explanation of the presence of heavy elements in abundance in the planets.

With the rejection of the long time scale for the age of the universe, the figure generally accepted at the present time (1960), and apparently supported by many lines of astronomical investigation, is from 3 to 5×10^9 years. This figure means, of course, different things according to the cosmological view we adopt. If the Lemaître hypothesis of an expanding universe is accepted and we suppose, with Gamow, that it was created by a primæval explosion of a 'super-atom', then the figure 3 to 5×10^9 represents the age of the entire cosmos. On the other hand, if we accept the steady state universe as being nearer the mark, then the age refers only to the age of our galaxy and its contents. Observational evidence, as we have remarked, is inconclusive. We may remember the

THE TWENTIETH CENTURY 183

dictum that if creation were a unique event, then it occurred in conditions with which we are unfamiliar, and which are, therefore, virtually unamenable to scientific investigation. The steady state universe makes no such demand, but does propose a continuous creation of elementary atomic particles by a process at present unknown.

Finally, we must turn to recent and highly important developments in the field of astronomical observation. Firstly it must be recalled that while Heinrich Hertz first detected 'radio' waves as far back as 1887, the practical development of radio techniques had to wait until Marconi invented the aerial wire or antenna for transmitting and receiving, and Ambrose Fleming in 1904 constructed and used the thermionic valve. The first fruit of radio in the purely scientific field was the discovery and investigation of part of the Earth's atmosphere which acts as a reflector to the majority of radio waves. This ionosphere, as the layers in this region came to be called, was found to be made up of layers of ionized air particles, the reflecting power and position of which have been seen to vary according to solar activity. It became clear that a watch kept on the ionosphere could assist in solar studies. The next step came in 1932, when Karl Jansky was investigating the subject of radio interference. Jansky noticed that radio 'noise'[1] appeared to come from within our own galaxy. Ten years later radio emission was discovered to emanate from the Sun. J. S. Hey found that noise of metre wavelengths appeared to be associated with sunspot activity, while G. C. Southworth found that there was also a steady noise emission on centimetre wavelengths. In 1944 G. Reber also discovered solar noise in metre wavelengths. The third discovery of basic importance was that of Hey who, in collaboration with G. S. Stewart, found that the

---

[1] The term 'noise' has a technical significance in radio engineering. It is used to refer to electrical energy with an almost continuous spectrum, in contrast with the discrete frequencies used in radio transmission.

paths of meteors could be tracked by radar techniques[1] which had been developed by Appleton and Watson-Watt. At the end of the second world war these early results led to developments of vast importance, and the radio telescope has come to be accepted as a new means of space-penetration. First results were obtained using an aerial system at the focus of a parabolic reflector and recently the world's largest instrument of this kind, with a parabola of 250-foot diameter, has been set up at Jodrell Bank near Manchester in England. However, instruments of considerable resolving power can be constructed using large aerial arrays with limited degrees of movement, but arranged as giant interferometers. Two-aerial systems can be wired to form an interferometer by 'mixing' the signals received in each aerial system so that the resolving power of one system can reinforce that of the other. Instruments of this kind have been designed and built by Little, McCready, Mills, Pawsey, Payne-Scott and Ryle. The radio telescope, in whatever form it takes, has proved in the few years of its existence to be a very powerful space-investigating tool. Unaffected by local weather conditions, and able to record its data automatically, it gives the astronomer, both professional and amateur, a new 'eye' with which to observe and map the universe. Investigations of the Sun have brought much new knowledge; in particular it has been possible to trace the solar corona out to distances where visually it cannot be discerned at all. Discrete sources have been found within our own galaxy and have enabled the astronomer to penetrate much dust and gas which acts as a screen to radiation at visual wavelengths. By radio means it has thus been possible to aid investigations on the spiral nature of our own galaxy and help provide proof that it is, in fact, of spiral form.

[1] It is important to appreciate the difference between *radio* and *radar* techniques. *Radio* astronomical investigation is concerned with the *receipt* of 'noise' from 'space', while *radar* is used for emitting radio pulses and receiving the echoes back from other bodies or from masses of ionized gas.

Many galactic radio sources have been referred to by the name *radio stars*. This is perhaps unfortunate because it is not clear that the sources so far mapped can be identified with stars which have been visually observed, while in certain instances the visual object has been found to be the shell of an old supernova. The term *radio source* now seems to be gaining favour, and this is to be welcomed, as it does not prejudge in our minds the nature of the emitter. Radio noise has also been discovered to be emitted by atomic hydrogen dispersed within the galaxy, while Lovell and his colleagues have done much to investigate meteors and meteoric dust. Thus the radio telescope has also proved itself to be of great use in the investigation of the galaxies external to our own, and it would seem that the space-penetrating power of these instruments may well make them particularly useful in investigations which may prove of vital importance in cosmological speculation.

While one of the 'glories' of the radio telescope is its independence of local weather conditions, attempts have also been made by the 'visual astronomer' to get over some of the problems which arise due to the comparatively thick atmosphere close to the Earth's surface. Dollfus of the Paris observatory is experimenting with telescopic observing techniques using a gas-filled balloon and by its means rising above low-lying dense atmosphere, while reference has already been made to the use of high-altitude observatories for studies of the solar prominences and corona. A new hope for the visual astronomer has come with the advent of instrumented rockets. Rocket techniques, pursued originally and primarily for military purposes, are now also used as a means for investigating the upper air and ionosphere. Work along these lines has been stimulated by the great international programme of research into the Earth as a physical body and known as the International Geophysical Year (1957–1958). Rocket design has now made it possible to send up rockets to heights at which the Earth's atmosphere has but a minor effect on the radiations from space. Because of technical developments in radio control and electronics in general, it is now practicable to send off instruments and receive from them radio signals which can be 'coded' to provide information on their readings of physical phenomena. There is still a great amount of work to be done in this field, but the first results have been very promising and augur well for the future, not least of these being the launching of artificial satellites which have assisted the astronomer in the problem which he has so often tackled, of measuring the shape of the Earth.

For generations man has dreamed and even written fiction about travelling into space. To say that space travel now seems possible is probably an understatement. Already certain nations are scientifically investigating the effects which such travel will have on the human frame, and designing clothing and conditions which will make it possible, ere long, to launch a human being into space. In the conceivable future it seems virtually certain that any human space travel will of necessity be confined to the Moon and the planets close to the Earth. Moreover, because of the immense distances involved, it would seem likely that space travel within our own galaxy may be subject to limitation.

The future of astronomy and of cosmology is bright with promise. If we look back, even in so incomplete a way as we have done in these pages, we can see the great strides which man has taken in understanding the vast and complex universe in which he finds himself. From the earliest times when nomadic peoples developed their ideas about the stars, the Sun and the Moon, mankind has learned the lesson of objective and quantitative study and, in more recent times, the importance in scientific activities of true international cooperation. Indeed in the field of international politics perhaps it is fair to claim that the scientist has lessons to teach the politician and the administrator. The journey from a flat

Earth and dome-like heaven created by gods and demi-gods to a steady state universe which, as a physical cosmos, had no beginning and has no end, has taken a long time. Each generation has built upon the ruins as well as the edifices created by those who have gone before. When one considers, even briefly, the advances which have been made and equates them with the tools of study that have been available at any time, the journey seems to be an exploration of immense boldness and grandeur. With a knowledge of what has gone before, of the achievements and the blind alleys, one is stimulated not only to gaze in wonder at the present amazing picture of the universe which is being formulated, but also to look ahead with expectation at what there is yet to learn and to appraise critically present results and future developments as they occur.

Appendix I

THE LUNAR AND SOLAR CALENDARS

In 433 B.C. Meton and Euctemon found that after a period of nineteen years, new moons and full moons recurred on the same days of the year. The reason for this is that 19 tropical years are almost exactly equal to an integral number of synodic months:

19 tropical years = 19 × 365·2422 days = 6939·60 days
and 235 synodic months = 235 × 29·5306 days = 6939·69 days

The error in this *Metonic Cycle* amounts then to 0·09 days per 19 years or 1 day in a little over 211 years.

In order to compute solar calendar dates for festivals kept by a lunar calendar, use is made of two concepts – the *Golden Number* and the *Epact*. The *Golden Number* for any year x A.D. is given by the remainder when $(1 + x)$ is divided by 19.

The *Epact* is the Moon's age on 1 January. Now twelve synodic months = 354·3672 days and differs from the tropical year by 10·8750 days or, to the nearest whole numbers, $\frac{11}{30}$ lunations. Hence we see that the Epact increases by $\frac{11}{30}$ of a lunation per year. Now the moon's age is always given as a fraction of a synodic month, that is whole months are not counted. Hence the Epact in days is given by

$$\frac{11 \,(\text{Golden Number} - 1)}{30}$$

As an example the Golden Number for 1960 is given by the remainder of $\frac{1960}{19}$ or 3. The Epact in days is then given by the remainder of $11\frac{(3-1)}{30}$ or 22. Thus the age of the Moon on 1 January 1960 was 22 days.

Appendix II

THE EPICYCLE AND DEFERENT AND THE MOVABLE ECCENTRIC

These two explanations offered to account for the motion of the outer planets using uniform circular motions are geometrically equivalent. This equivalence can be seen from the following diagram (fig. 8).

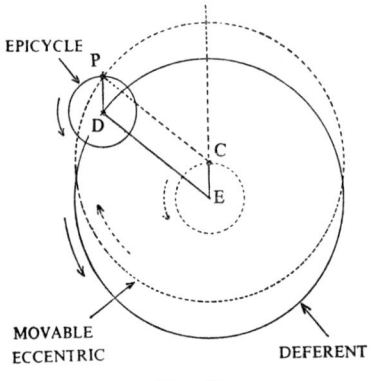

FIG. 8

P represents a planet, E the Earth. If the radius ED of the deferent is equal to CP (which is the radius of the eccentric), and if the radius EC of the concentric circle is equal to DP (the radius of the epicycle), then motion described by the deferent and epicycle may be equally well described using the movable eccentric. It should, however, be noted that this equivalence is only valid in respect of the planets Mars, Jupiter and Saturn, i.e. those planets whose orbits lie, on a heliocentric hypothesis, outside the orbit of the Earth. For the planets Mercury and Venus this equivalence is not valid. The series of figures (fig. 9a, b and c) show this similarity in a graphic manner.

It may be of interest to note that the term *epicycle* is derived from two Greek words, ἐπί – upon, and κύκλος – a circle. It is really very descriptive – an 'upon-circle'. The term *deferent* is derived from the Latin *defero* to carry, and its use here will be obvious.

APPENDIX II

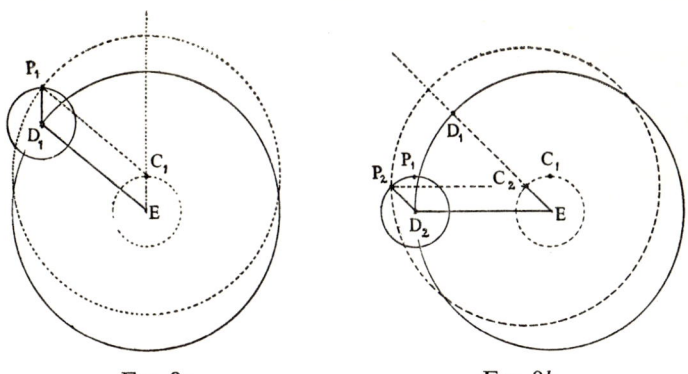

Fig. 9a   Fig. 9b

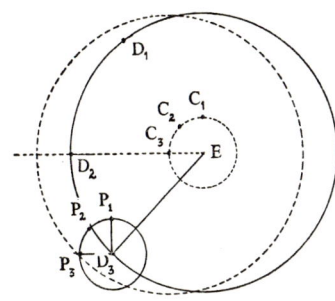

Fig. 9c

Appendix III

A NOTE ON THE HARMONY OF THE UNIVERSE

According to the Pythagorean outlook everything was governed by numerical relationships. They knew the relationships between the sounds on a particular musical scale, using the two segments of a stretched string, the lengths of the segments being in a simple numerical ratio. The Pythagorean musical scale was similar to our present tempered major scale. Aristotle in *De Cælo* reported that the Pythagoreans believed that the various heavenly revolutions produced different tones which we cannot hear because we have become so accustomed to them, having heard them from birth.

Pliny the Younger in his *Historia Naturalis* claimed that the planetary intervals were as follows:

Earth	
	whole tone
Moon	
	semitone
Mercury	
	semitone
Venus	
	minor third
Sun	
	whole tone
Mars	
	semitone
Jupiter	
	semitone
Saturn	
	minor third
Fixed Stars	

or as expressed in musical notation

Other writers gave slight variations.

APPENDIX III

Kepler in his *Harmonices Mundi libri V* sought for a scale giving perfect consonance and considered not the distances of the planets from each other but, instead, their greatest and least orbital velocities, i.e. their velocities at perihelion and aphelion. Taking the daily motion in seconds of arc Kepler obtained:

	"
Saturn	108
	135
Jupiter	270
	330
Mars	1521
	2281
Earth	3448
	3678
Venus	5690
	5927
Mercury	9840
	23640

Kepler analysed these figures by considering the ratios of aphelion to perihelion velocities and then, by using factors of 2 as divisors, he arranged the ratios to give notes on the untempered scale. By present standards Kepler's development of his ideas is rather complex. However, the results may be obtained without difficulty if we take the values for aphelion and perihelion velocities, and reduce them by some factor which will allow the aphelion velocity for Saturn to be equated to a frequency of a low note on the tempered scale. We shall then find that the other values may also be equated to the frequencies in cycles per second for other notes.

Thus for Saturn we have:

| aphelion velocity | 108" |
| perihelion velocity | 135" |

Dividing both by the factor 4·4 we obtain:

| aphelion velocity | 24·5 |
| perihelion velocity | 30·7 |

and 24·5 is the frequency of the note

and 30·7 the frequency of the note

Dealing in the same way with the remaining values of aphelion and perihelion velocities we obtain the following ranges:

SATURN   JUPITER   MARS   EARTH   VENUS   MERCURY

Because the variation in angular velocity varies from aphelion (minimum) to perihelion (maximum) and back to aphelion (minimum), we can fill in the intervals between the lowest and highest notes and thus form musical scales. For example the 'scale' for Mars can be represented as:

Kepler himself looked on this matter of harmony from a mathematical viewpoint. An examination of the planetary 'scales' indicates, in a graphic manner, the eccentricities of the planetary orbits and the 'gap' between Jupiter and Mars is clearly indicated.

Appendix IV

TRANSITS OF PLANETS AND DETERMINATION OF THE ASTRONOMICAL UNIT

If the Sun is at S (fig. 10) and the Earth at E then the planets Mercury and Venus will be seen to transit across the face of the Sun by an observer at O, when the planet is at P. An observer at O' will, however, only see a transit beginning when the planet has reached P'. If OO' is known and also the distance of the planet from the Earth, then, using Kepler's law relating the planetary period with its mean distance from the Sun, it is possible to compute the distance Earth to Sun and thus obtain the astronomical unit a.

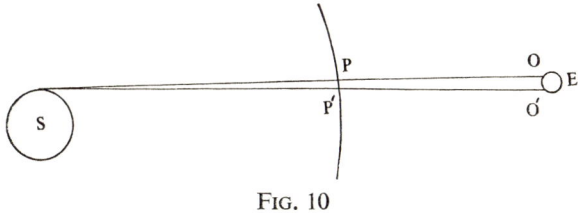

Fig. 10

Because Venus approaches more closely to the Earth than does Mercury, the distance Earth to Venus can be obtained more accurately than the distance Earth to Mercury. Hence the use of transits of Venus for determining a is more accurate than using transits of Mercury. However, transits of Venus are rare; they can occur in pairs 8 years apart but the interval between such pairs (and often between each transit) is about 243 years, whereas transits of Mercury may be repeated at intervals of either 7, 12 or 46 years. In spite of the rarity of transits of Venus, their use for determining a is to be recommended in preference to using transits of Mercury.

Appendix V

THE CELESTIAL SPHERE

The celestial sphere is that sphere with the Earth at its centre upon which the stars and planets can be projected.

The CELESTIAL EQUATOR is the projection on to the celestial sphere of the terrestrial equator.

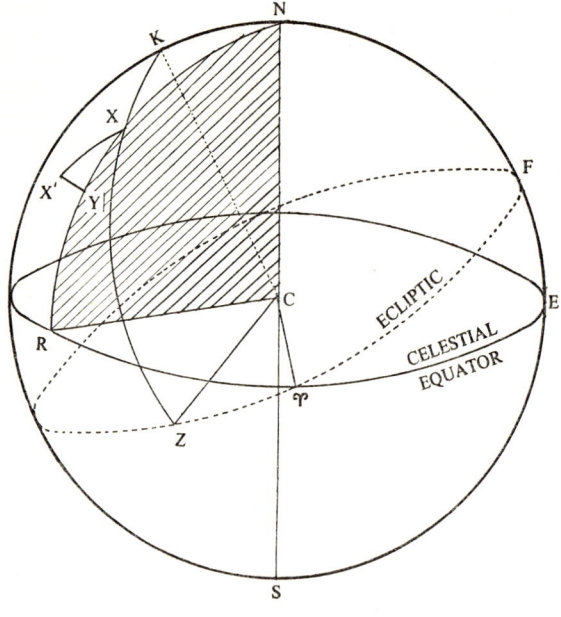

FIG. 11

THE CELESTIAL POLES (N. and S.) are the projection on to the celestial sphere of the geographical poles of the Earth (fig. 11).

The ECLIPTIC is the projection on the celestial sphere of the Sun's path.

The FIRST POINT OF ARIES (♈) is at one of the points of intersection of the *ecliptic* and the *celestial equator*.

APPENDIX V

RIGHT ASCENSION is the equivalent on the celestial sphere of *terrestrial longitude* and is measured *westwards* along the *celestial equator* starting at the *first point of Aries*. Thus the right ascension of the star X is the angle ♈CR.

DECLINATION is the equivalent on the celestial sphere of *terrestrial latitude*. It is measured as + when *north of the celestial equator* and − when south. Thus the declination of the star X is + and is given by the angle RCX.

CELESTIAL LONGITUDE and CELESTIAL LATITUDE are measured with respect to the ecliptic and the pole of the ecliptic (K). Thus the celestial longitude of the star X is given by the angle ♈CZ and the *celestial latitude* by the angle ZCX.

The OBLIQUITY OF THE ECLIPTIC is given by the angle E♈F. The PROPER MOTION of a star is the motion against a background of apparently non-moving stars. It is measured in *right ascension* (YX′) and in *declination* (XY). The proper motion is the resultant (XX′).

The PARALLAX of a star is a measure of its distance. There are a number of criteria for providing the parallax of a star. The first measures made of stellar parallax were *trigonometrical*. The diameter of the Earth's orbit is used as base line (EE′) and the *parallax* is the angle π (fig. 12).

Fig. 12

BIBLIOGRAPHY

The following selected books are recommended for further reading, while it may also be noted that papers on the history of astronomy appear from time to time in certain periodicals, a selective list of which is also given.

(I) *Greek and Early Astronomy*

DREYER, J. L. E.	*History of Planetary Systems from Thales to Kepler*[1]	London	1906
HEATH, T. L.	*Greek Astronomy*	London	1932
NEUGEBAUR, O.	*Astronomical Cuneiform Texts* (3 vols.)		1955
	The Exact Sciences in Antiquity	Princeton	1952
SARTON, G.	*History of Science*	London	1953

(II) *Medieval Astronomy*

CROMBIE, A. C.	*Augustine to Galileo*	London	1952
THORNDYKE, L.	*A History of Magic and Experimental Science during the First Thirteen Centuries of Our Era* (2 vols.)		1923

(III) *Modern and General Histories of Astronomy and Science*

ABETTI, G.	*A History of Astronomy*	London	1954
BUTTERFIELD, H.	*Origins of Modern Science*	London	1949
CLERKE, A.	*A Popular History of Astronomy during the Nineteenth Century*	London	1902
DAMPIER, W. C. D.	*A History of Science*	London	1942
DELAMBRE, J.	*Histoire de l'Astronomie au dix-huitième siècle*	Paris	1827
	Histoire de l'Astronomie Moderne (2 vols.)	Paris	1821
DOIG, P.	*A Concise History of Astronomy*	London	1950
KING, H. C.	*History of the Telescope*	London	1955
PINGRÉ, A. G.	*Annales Célestes du dix-huitième siècle*	Paris	1901
PLEDGE, H. T.	*Science since 1500*	London	1939

[1] Also published by Dover Publications, New York, in 1953 under the title *History of Astronomy*.

BIBLIOGRAPHY

SHAPLEY, H. and HOWARTH, H.	*Source Book in Astronomy*	New York	1929
WATERFIELD, R. L.	*Hundred Years of Astronomy*	London	1938
WOOLF, H.	*Transits of Venus*	Princeton	1959

(IV) *Philosophy of Science*

| BURTT, E. A. | *The Metaphysical Foundations of Modern Physical Science* | London | 1932 |
| DINGLE, H. | *The Scientific Adventure* | London | 1952 |

(V) *Biographies*

ANDRADE, E. N. DA C.	*Isaac Newton*	London	1950
ARMITAGE, A.	*Copernicus*	London	1938
ARMITAGE, A. and RONAN, C. A.	*Edmond Halley*	London	1956
CASPAR, M.	*Kepler*	London	1959
DOUGLAS, V.	*Arthur Stanley Eddington*	London	1956
DREYER, J. L. E.	*Tycho Brahe*	London	1890
FAHIE, J. J.	*Galileo, His Life and Work*	London	1903
HISTORY OF SCIENCE SOCIETY	*Johann Kepler*	Baltimore	1931
MCPIKE, E. F.	*Correspondence and Papers of Edmond Halley*		
	Hevelius, Flamsteed and Halley	London	1937
MORE, L. T.	*Isaac Newton*	New York	1934
SCHILPP (editor)	*Albert Einstein: Philosopher and Scientist*	Illinois	1949
SCOTT, J. F. and TURNBULL, H. W.	The Correspondence of Isaac Newton (7 vols.) Vol. I 1959 Vol. II 1960 Vols. III–VII in preparation	London	

(VI) *Periodicals*

Annals of Science	London
Archives Internationales d'Histoire des Sciences	Paris
Centaurus	Copenhagen
Isis	Washington
Journal of the British Astronomical Association	London
Notes and Records of the Royal Society	London
Osiris	Belgium
Revue d'Histoire des Sciences	Paris

INDEX

aberration of starlight, 116, 149
absolute magnitude, 158
Abul Wefa, 79
accuracy in observing,
  by Flamsteed, 131
  by Tycho, 94
  by photographic means, 146
Adams, J. C., 154
Adams, W. S., 172
æther, velocity of the Earth in, 150
air, Empedocles on nature of, 46
Airy, 148
Al-Battani, 78, 79, 81
d'Alembert, 117, 119
Alexandrian library, destruction of, 76, 77
Al Hakim, 80
Alkarizmi, 80, 81
Almagest, 70, 78
alphabet, beginnings of, 39
Alter, D., 140
Amorites, 25
Anaxagoras, 47, 48
Anaximander, 42
Anaximenes, 43
Ångström, 142
annual equation of the Moon's orbit, 95
Apollonius, 64, 65
Arabic astronomy, 77–81
'Arabic' numerals, 80
Archer, 145
Argelander, 152, 153
Aristarchus, 64–6
Aristotle, 61–3, 82
Assyrian astronomical texts, 27
asteroids, 154
astrology,
  and Alexandria, 76

astrology and Babylonia, 27
  and Western Christendom, 81
astronomical unit, *see under* Sun, distance of
'atomic' theory of Democritus and Leucippus, 53–5

Baade, 177
Babylonia,
  its astronomy, 24–31
  its mathematics, 28, 29
Bacon, F., 109
Benedetti, 103
Bennett, 146
Bentley, 115
Berosus, 30
Berthe, 181
Bessel, 151
Biot, 156
Bolyai, F. (jnr), 170
Bolyai, F. (snr), 170
Bond, 144
Bondi, 180
Borelli, 108
Bradley, 116, 117, 125, 148, 149
Brahe, *see under* Tycho
Brewster, 140
Bruno, 88–91, 103
Bunsen, 140, 141

Calendars, lunar and solar, 189
  in Babylonia, 27
  in Egypt, 33, 34
  and the Greeks, 44, 60
  in Mexico, 22
  in prehistory, 14
Cassegrain, 125, 127
Cassini (Cesare), 130
Cassini (Giacomo), 130

INDEX

Cassini (Gian Domenico), 129, 130, 147
celestial bodies and uniform circular motion, 51
celestial sphere, 196, 197
Cepheid variables, 166, 175, 177
Chandrasekhar, 181
Charlier, 168
Chinese astronomy, 18–20
Clairaut, 117, 119
Cleostratus, 43, 44
clepsydræ, 45
comets,
  and the Babylonians, 28
  and the Chinese, 19
  and fifteenth-century observations, 83
  and the Greeks, 62, 74, 75
  and Halley, 115, 116, 156
  and meteors, 156, 157
  and Newton, 114, 156
  and Tycho, 94
Comte, 121, 140
constellations,
  Egyptian, 33
  Greek, 39, 44
  Mexican, 21
continuous creation of matter, 180
Copernican theory, 85–8
  in England, 91
  and religious objections to 86–8
Copernicus, 84–8
coronagraph, 163
cosmology,
  Egyptian, 34, 35
  Greek, 40, 57
  twentieth-century hypotheses of, 169–75, 177–83
counter-earth, 52
Crabtree, 102
crystalline spheres, 60, 61

Daguerre, 143
Darwin, 159

Davy, 143, 144
Dee, 91
deification of celestial bodies,
  by Babylonians, 26
  by Mexicans, 23
Democritus, 53–5
Descartes, 106–8
Deslandres, 163
Digges, (Leonard), 125
Digges, (Thomas), 91, 93, 94, 125
Dirac, 177
Dollfus, 185
Dollond, 135
dome-shaped heavens,
  and the Babylonians, 31
  and the Mexicans, 23
  in prehistory, 15, 16
Doppler, 141
Draper, 142, 159
dynamical astronomy, 98–123

Earth,
  concept of flatness of, 41–3, 48, 82
  concept of as stationary, 61
  diurnal motion of and the Greeks, 63, 64
  orbital motion of and the Greeks, 65
  spherical shape of, 51, 57
  size of, 62, 66, 67
eclipses, Greek views on, 46, 47
ecliptic, obliquity of,
  and the Greeks, 43
  and the Mexicans, 22
Eddington, 160, 173, 177–81
Egyptian astronomy, 31–6
Einstein, 169–75
elements,
  and Aristotle, 63
  and Empedocles, 45
  and Leucippus and Democritus, 53–5
Empedocles, 45–6
Encke, 148

INDEX

epicycles, 64, 65, 70–4, 190, 191
equant, 73
Eratosthenes, 66, 67
Euclid, 56
Euctemon, 189
Eudoxus, 59, 60
Euler, 117–19
Evershed, 162
evolution, 159, 160

Field, J., 91
fire, concept of as primeval substance, 44
fixed eccentric, 68
Fizeau, 141, 149
Fitzgerald, 168
Flamsteed, 130, 131
Foucault, 139, 140, 148, 149
Fraunhofer, 139
Fresnel, 150

the Galaxy, 161
galaxies, 165, 166
Galileo, 98, 102–6, 127, 128
Galle, 155
Gamow, 181
Gascoigne, 126
Gauss, 170
Generini, 126
geometry,
   non-Euclidean, 170–1
   Pythagorean, 50
Gerbert, 82
Gill, 147, 148
gravitation, 113, 114
Greek astronomy, 37–75
Greek learning and the West, 79
Greek migrations, 37, 39
Greenwich observatory, 130–2
Gregory, J., 125–7
Guinaud, 135

Hale, 163
Hall, 135

Halley, 110, 111, 113, 115, 116, 132–4, 147, 151, 156, 167
Hammurabi, 25
Haroun-al-Rashid, 78
Harriott, 124
Harrison, 134
heliacal risings and settings, 15
helium, identification of, 143
Henderson, 151
Heracleides, 63, 64
Heracleitus, 44–6
Hertz, 172, 183
Hertzsprung, 158, 159
Herschel, J., 139, 142, 144, 145, 152, 153, 155
Herschel, W., 122, 136–8, 142, 152, 153
Hesiod, 39
Hevelius, 126
Hey, 183, 184
Hinks, 165
Hipparchus, 67–9, 76
Homer, 40
homocentric spheres of Eudoxus, 60
Hooke, 110, 113
Horrox, 102
Hoyle, 180, 181
Hubble, 175, 177
Huggins, 142, 146, 158
Humason, 175, 176, 177
Huygens, 128, 129, 150

Indian astronomy, 20
Ionians, 40, 41
Islamic astronomy, 77–81

Jansky, 183
Jeans, 181, 182

Kant, 120–2
Kapteyn, 161
Kepler, 98–103
Kirchhoff, 140, 141
Kugler, 24

Lacaille, 153
Lagrange, 118, 119
Lalande, 153
Lambert, 121, 122
Laplace, 119–22
Lassell, 137, 154, 155
Leavitt, 166
Lemaître, 180
Leucippus, 53, 54
Leverrier, 148, 154, 171, 172
Levi-Civita, 171
light, velocity of, 149, 168
Lippershey, 125
Little, 184
Lobatchewski, 170
Lockyer, 141, 142, 156, 157
Lodge, 150, 169
longitude, determination of, 133, 134
Lorentz, 168, 170
Lyot, 163
Lyttleton, 180

Maddox, 146
Maestlin, 98
Maksutov, 176
Marconi, 183
Maskelyne, 137, 153
Maxwell, 172
McCrea, 180
McCready 184
McVittie, 179
Menzel, 163
Mercury, transits of, 148, 195
meridian arc, measurement of length of, 130
Messier, 153
meteors, 156, 157
Meton, 189
Mexican astronomy, 21–4
Michelson, 150, 168
Milky Way,
  and Anaxagoras, 48
  and Aristotle, 63
  Mexican views, 21

Mills, 184
Milne, 179, 180
Minkowski, 170
Minoan civilization, 37
Molyneux, 148
Moon,
  distance of, 65, 66
  first photograph of, 145
  nature of, Greek views on, 42, 45
  orbital motion of, 103, 113, 117
  surface of, 84, 127
Montanari, 126
Morley, 150, 168
motion of bodies,
  and Galileo, 103
  and Newton, 112, 113
movable excentric, 64, 65, 190, 191
Muller, 83
music of the spheres, 51, 52, 101, 192–4

Nasmyth, 155
Nassir-al-Din, 79
'natural' place of material substances, 42
nebulae, 153, 165
nebular hypothesis (Kant and Laplace), 121
Neugebauer, 24, 29, 35
Newton, 110–15, 125, 127, 138, 150, 156, 157
Nicholas of Cusa, 83, 84
Niepce, 143
numbers, Pythagorean, 49, 50
nutation, 118, 119

Olbers, 167, 168
Omar, 77
Oort, 161
Origen, 81
Osiander, 85–7

π, value of, 28

INDEX

papyrus, invention of, 32
Paris observatory, 129, 130
Pawsey, 184
Payne-Scott, 184
Pericles, 47
Philolaus, 52, 53
Phœnicians, 39
photography, early development of, 143–7
Piazzi, 154
Picard, 130
Plato, 56–8
Pogson, 152, 153
precession, 95
prehistory of astronomy, 13–17
the *Principia*, 111–14
proper motions of stars, 151
Ptolemaic system, 71–4
Ptolemy, 27, 69–74, 76, 79, 82
'Ptolemy's rules', 71, 72
Purbach, 83
Pythagoras, 48–52

quantum theory, 177

radio-astronomy, 183–5
Reber, 183
Recorde, 91
red-shift, 141, 142, 167
Regiomontanus, 83
relativity, 169–75, 177–81
Richer, 130
Riefler, 163
Riemann, 170–1
Ritz, 168
rocket-astronomy, 185–6
Roman Catholic Church,
  and Copernican theory, 86–8, 105–6
  and Galileo, 104–6
Römer, 125, 126, 129, 149
Rosse, Earl of, 136, 137
Rosseland, 181
Rowland, 142
Royal Society, 109–10

de la Rue, 145
Russell, Bertrand, 49
Russell, H. N., 159, 160
Ryle, 184

Sacrobosco, 82
St Ambrose, 77
St Cyril, 76
St Thomas Aquinas, 82
Sarton, 25, 32, 39, 41
Saturn, rings of, 128
Scheele, 143
Scheiner, 155
Schiaparelli, 156
Schmidt, 176
Schultze, 143
Schwabe, 155
Secchi, 141
Seleucid mathematics, 29
Seleucids, 26
Shapley, 166
de Sitter, 168, 180
Slipher, 175, 176
Socrates, 20, 56
Sola, 143
solar system, formation of, 122, 123, 181
solar telescopes, 162
spectrohelioscope, 163
spectroscopy, 138–143
spectrum, extra-visual range of, 142
Spencer Jones, 165
stadium, size of, 62
star-atlas, first one produced by photography, 146
star-catalogues, 67, 71, 95, 130–2
stellar constitution, 181
stellar distribution, 153
stellar evolution, 159, 160
stellar magnitudes, 152
stellar motions, 161
stellar parallax, 151
Stewart, 183
Southworth, 183

Stoics, 66
Stokes, 140
Struve, 148, 151
Sumerian astronomy, 26
Sumerian civilization, 25
Sumerian mathematics, 28
Sun,
    distance of, 65, 66, 68, 123, 147, 148, 165
    first photograph of, 144
    nature of, Greek ideas on, 42, 45
sundials, 18, 29, 30, 34
sunspots, 155, 162, 163

Tabit-ben-Korra, 78, 79, 95
Talbot, 144, 145
Taupendt, 146
telescope,
    achromatic, 134, 135
    advent of large reflectors, 162
    equatorial mounting of, 126
    invention of, 124, 125
    and Galileo, 104, 125
    reflecting, 125–7, 136, 137, 161, 162
    refracting, 124–6, 134–6
Tempel, 156
Thales, 40–1, 43
Theophilus, 76
timekeeping, accuracy in, 163–5
Toscanelli, 83, 84
trepidation of the Moon, 78, 95
trigonometry and Islam, 80
Trumpler, 167
Tycho Brahe, 63, 92–6, 98, 99

Ulugh Beg, 78, 80
universe,
    age of, 181, 182
    infinite extent of, 120–2, 133, 167, 168, 177, 178
    twentieth-century concepts of, 169–75, 177–83
Unsöld, 181

variation of the Moon's orbit, 79, 95
Venus, transits of, 102, 147, 148, 195
da Vinci, 84
Vogel, 142, 158
vortex theory, 47, 107

Walther, 83
water, concept of as primeval substance, 41
Wedgwood, 143, 144
Weizsäcker, 181
Wilson, 154
Wolf, 154
Wollaston, 139
Woolley, Sir Leonard, 25
Wren, 110, 113, 130
Wright, 120

Young, 150

zero, use of, 28, 80
zodiac,
    Babylonian, 30
    Chinese, 18, 19
    Greek, 44

INDIAN RIVER JUNIOR COLLEGE LIBRARY
FORT PIERCE, FLORIDA